UNLESS SOMEONE SHOWS ME

English grammar for students of biblical languages

JOHN A. DAVIES

WIPF & STOCK · Eugene, Oregon

Wipf and Stock Publishers
199 W 8th Ave, Suite 3
Eugene, OR 97401

Unless Someone Shows Me
English Grammar for Students of Biblical Languages
By Davies, John
Copyright©2013 Morning Star Publishing
ISBN 13: 978-1-4982-3010-0
Publication date 4/30/2015
Previously published by Morning Star Publishing, 2013

Contents

Preface

Of the making of grammar books there is no end! What contribution then does this one seek to make? Grammar books can be written with a number of objectives, such as to provide a manual of correct usage or good style or to teach English as a second language. While there might be some indirect benefit in these areas, these are not the primary aims of this book. This book is designed for students embarking on the exciting venture of learning another language, specifically one of the major biblical languages, Hebrew and Greek. However, there is not a Hebrew or Greek word to be found in these pages (unless it has been adopted as an English word), and only in passing is there mention of Hebrew and Greek grammatical concepts by way of comparison with English. This book is about the way language in general, and English in particular works, since a knowledge of English grammar is to some extent assumed as a basis for learning the target languages. What exactly is a verb? What does passive mean? Why do we have different words for *she* and *her*? What is a relative clause?

While they may give a brief definition of grammatical terms and how they apply in English, textbooks of biblical languages sometimes proceed too quickly on the assumption that students generally have this on board. In the textbooks, material is introduced in an order which suits the pedagogy of the target language. As a consequence, students often have no broad architectural conception of how their own language works. This book is written to fill that gap.

This grammar then (unlike most modern English grammars) has written English in view rather than its spoken form, as the target languages are preserved via written texts and the comparisons made and the translations you will be required to produce in due course will largely be written. Consequently this book would be useful with little adaptation for students of Latin or any ancient language, particularly an inflected language — those learned largely from textbooks.

This book, while informed by more recent linguistic insights, adopts a modified traditional grammatical framework since most textbooks of Hebrew and Greek work with more or less traditional grammatical categories. I have tried to avoid complex diagrams and abbreviations. Students have enough ahead of them learning Hebrew or Greek without having to learn the obscure language of grammatical coding. As with any discipline a certain amount of terminology is needed, and the technical labels are introduced and defined and illustrated. Not every textbook uses precisely the same technical terms. Care has been taken to work through quite a number of the textbooks in use and to use alternative descriptive labels where this would be helpful.

Just as we see our own culture in a new light when we travel abroad, it is my hope that as you embark on learning another language, you will see things in a fresh light in English, appreciating more of its richness and subtlety. I trust that this book will be a useful guide on the journey.

I acknowledge my gratitude to my former teachers who inspired in me a love of language and to my students over forty years who have echoed the Ethiopian official's sentiments, if not in so many words, 'How can I understand unless someone shows me?' (Acts 8:31).

John A. Davies

June 2013

How to Use this Book

This book may be used in several ways. It may be used as a guide for preparatory study as a prelude to learning one or both or the major biblical languages, perhaps as a textbook for a short intensive course. Others may prefer to work through relevant chapters or sections concurrently with the study of particular topics in Hebrew or Greek. Teachers might give guidance on which sections would be most pertinent at any stage. Even students working through an intermediate grammar of Hebrew or Greek may find it useful to consolidate their understanding of the relevant sections of topics in English grammar. The index may facilitate in the treatment of this as a reference guide for ongoing consultation.

Some points of comparison with Hebrew and Greek grammatical patterns are included, mainly to assist students in forming a conception of the similarities and differences across languages and the most basic of orientations to the issues to be encountered in the biblical languages. These are generally in a smaller font and may be skipped if preferred without loss of continuity to the discussion of English grammar.

In grammar, everything is connected to everything else. It is difficult to discuss the functions of nouns except in relation to verbs, or participles except in relation to adjectives. Some reference, therefore, to grammatical features yet to be dealt with in greater detail is inevitable. The frequent cross-referencing throughout (using the hierarchical system of sections set out in the contents and marked with the § mark) draws the reader's attention to where a term (generally highlighted by **bold type**) is introduced or primarily defined and illustrated, whether that is in a previous section or a later section. This, along with the index, should make it relatively easy to find the topic you are looking for and make this a serviceable reference book for later consultation when greater detail on the finer points is called for.

It will be helpful if the reader understands a few of the conventions employed in this book. The asterisk (*) is used before non-standard ('ungrammatical') forms or expressions. The plus sign (+) means 'followed by or together with'. The plus or minus sign (±) means 'optionally followed by or together with'. *Italic* font is used for examples and the key elements under consideration in an example may be highlighted by <u>underlining</u>.

Many of the examples used in the following pages will have a familiar ring to students of the Bible. However, these have sometimes been simplified so as to remove matter extraneous to the point being illustrated, so Bible references are not given unless for a specific purpose such as comparing translations or drawing attention to grammatical forms now considered archaic.

The exercises at the end of each chapter (with answers at the back) are designed to get you thinking about how language does what it sets out to do — to communicate, even across thousands of years. Some of the questions are designed to be challenging and some could arguably be answered in a different way. The point is to stimulate conscious reflection on our use of language. Treat any 'wrong' answers as a learning experience (some explanations are given in the answers) and an opportunity to revisit the relevant section to gain a better understanding of the topic under consideration.

Abbreviations

CGEL   *The Cambridge Grammar of the English Language,* by Rodney Huddleston and Geoffrey K. Pullum (Cambridge: Cambridge University Press, 2002)

HCSB   The Holman Christian Standard Bible

KJV   King James Version of the Bible

Message   The Message: The Bible in Contemporary English

NEB   The New English Bible

NET   The NET Bible (New English Translation)

NIV2011   The New International Version of the Bible, 2011 edition

NLT   The New Living Translation of the Bible, Second edition

NRSV   The New Revised Standard Version of the Bible

1. Introduction: Grammar Is Not a Life Sentence

§1.1 Language Acquisition and Analysis

Our ability to communicate via language is a great gift and like any gift we should not take it for granted. How does language do what it does? How often do we look at it closely and think about what it is that enables us to speak and write original sentences? Or how we can understand what others have said or written? Of course we will have an idea of how words represent things, but words without a structure are a meaningless string of unrelated items. Most of the sentences we hear or read have never been said or written before but we do not generally struggle to decode their meaning. We instinctively know the difference between:

Your enemies will pursue you.

and:

You will pursue your enemies.

even though these sentences use exactly the same words. We intuitively know that *purple cloth* sounds right but **cloth purple* does not. It is the stuff of grammar to talk about how words do their work in cooperation with each other.

A common lament of those learning another language, such as Hebrew or Greek, that 'I never learned English grammar' cannot be entirely true. We all have a grammatical framework in our head, whether we are able to describe it or not. In the case of the sentences and phrases above, it is the ability to distinguish between subjects and objects and to know the function and position of adjectives in relation to their nouns, whether or not we have ever heard the words 'subject', 'object', 'adjective' or 'noun'.

Our first language is acquired by immersion in a linguistic environment through observation, imitation and analogy. Like walking, it is second nature once we have achieved a level of competence (which for most is well-developed by age three). There are different ways of acquiring a second language, but for most students of the ancient languages used in biblical studies, this is going to be not by deep immersion in the linguistic environment (native speakers of these languages are hard to come by!), but by textbook and classroom or online learning, and the focus is primarily on the corpus of written texts rather than on speech. What many of us do lack is a way of analysing and describing our language, so to be told that in the first example above the words *your enemies* form the subject and *you* the object may not mean much. What we need to do as a stepping stone to learning the new language is to acquire some facility with the system and terminology for analysing and discussing the way we use words: the system we call grammar.

§1.2 What Is Grammar? A Broad Definition

The word **grammar** is used in different ways. Many language textbooks describe themselves as *Grammars*. In this sense, the word is being used broadly to cover all aspects (at an elementary level at least) needed for the study of the language. This will include (for Hebrew and Greek) elements such as phonology (the sound system), the script and some vocabulary (word lists with simple English equivalents or **glosses**). In a more restricted sense, 'grammar' refers to the different forms these words may take and the ways they may be put together to form sentences. A further more extended use of the word is to describe a structure or set of 'rules' by which discourse (paragraphs or larger units of speech or text) is composed, or whole disciplines operate (the 'grammar of music').

It is more in the second sense above that this book uses the word grammar, though to be helpful, brief sections on phonology (sounds) and semantics (words and their meanings) follow.

§1.2.1 Phonology

Every language chooses a limited number of sounds from the very large number of sounds the human speech organs are capable of producing and the ear capable of distinguishing. Those sounds which impede the flow of air (or briefly stop it altogether) are the **consonants**; those that merely reshape the mouth for different resonances but do not impede the flow are the **vowels**, represented in English by (combinations of) *a, e, i, o, u* and sometimes *y*. The sounds a language community selects as making a meaningful difference are called **phonemes**. Thus the sounds represented by *l* and *r* are distinct phonemes in English (though not in some other languages), because *law* and *raw* have different meanings. However, the two different *t* sounds in *top* and *stop* are not separate phonemes; there are no words where the substitution of one *t* for the other would make a meaning difference, so most English speakers do not hear them as separate sounds (which they are in some languages).

> Hebrew has some sounds not regarded as phonemes by English speakers (e.g. its gutteral or throaty sounds) and originally distinguished between two *t* sounds and several *s* sounds. Greek has a *ch* (as in Scottish loch) which is phonemic in only some English dialects.

§1.2.2 Semantics: What Is a Word and What Does It Mean?

What is a word? Is *heartfelt* or *mother-in-law* or *Beth Shemesh* to be regarded as one word or more? Are *go* and *went* forms of the same word or different words? Here it would be useful to start to introduce some definitions which will help clarify things. These are not the only definitions or descriptive systems possible. The point is not to 'argue about words' (2 Tim 2:14) but to become comfortable with the broad contours of the descriptive framework commonly in use.

So let's begin with the 'word'. 'Word' is a non-technical, hence somewhat fuzzy, description of the labels we use to refer to things. A more technical category is the **lexeme** which is the grouping of related forms of what we think of as essentially the same 'word' when we go to look up a dictionary. Thus the verb forms *think, thinks, thinking* and *thought* constitute one lexeme. We conventionally select one form, the simplest, *THINK* (note the use of capitals) as the **lemma** or dictionary entry form. However, the related or **cognate** noun forms *thought* (as in *I had a thought*) and (plural) *thoughts* belong to a different lexeme, listed under the lemma *THOUGHT*.

One of the first things that students of other languages come to realise is that languages do not divide up our experience of the world into exactly the same conceptual categories. It is important to realise that the vocabulary lists in your language textbook can only provide a simple gloss or two for each entry — approximations that will suffice for the time being, but which do not convey the full range of possible meaning. Words often defy precise definition, let alone one-to-one equivalence across languages. We can only approach a definition asymptotically, i.e. getting closer to it the more examples of its use we consider and the more therefore we can observe its **semantic range** or **semantic domain**, the range or circle of meaning the word is normally capable of bearing. Thus the word *fruit* generally refers to (has as its typical **referent** or point of contact in the real or imagined world) a considerable range of edible (often sweet) seed-bearing tissue of flowering plants. But (in botanical terms) it may include also inedible matter and edible but not sweet vegetables such as pumpkin or tomato. It can also be used in more extended or metaphorical ways to refer to the product or result of something:

The _fruit_ of the Spirit is love, joy, peace ...

Some discussions make a distinction between a word's **denotation** or core meaning, and its possible **connotations** or extended meanings. It may be better simply to think of a **prototypical** meaning (the meaning we commonly think of) and a fuzzy range of possible extensions of that meaning, some of which may become relatively commonplace, others of which might only be used once for startling effect.

As noted above, some lemmas belong in a family of cognate words, i.e. they share a semantic domain and a common core or **root** (even if it has undergone some changes to produce the various lemmas). Thus *just, justify, justification, justly* and *unjust* share a semantic domain and have underlying their various forms the root element *just*. The root might be an abstraction, not realised as a lemma itself. The roots of *uncouth* and *unruly* are the unused forms (unless for humorous effect) *couth and *ruly. Whether or not we are aware of the history of the words, we sense this since we recognise the prefix *un-* as a negator (§6.1).

> The discussion of a word's root assumes greater prominence in the study of Greek and particularly Hebrew. One of the standard **lexicons** or dictionaries of Hebrew lists all words under their supposed root.

Just because English uses a word like *fruit* with a particular set of typical and extended meanings, it does not follow that the word used in Hebrew or Greek with a roughly similar prototypical meaning will have the same range of extended meanings (though there may in fact be considerable overlap). We mentally group items together because they have (as we and our language community conventionally envisage them) similar features and attributes. The word *house* refers to members of a class that includes a range of styles of building for human habitation (as distinct from a natural cave dwelling), normally relatively permanent and of fixed location (as distinct from a tent, caravan etc.), and then by extension other buildings (*the house of the Lord*) and some more abstract notions (*the house of Saul, a spiritual house*). *Delight* refers to a response towards one end of the spectrum of possible responses of sentient beings to a range of stimuli — sight, sound, smell, mental stimuli, etc., but pinning it down precisely in its relation to *satisfaction, pleasure, joy, elation* or *ecstasy* would not be easy.

Of course speakers of another language may categorise things and experiences rather differently. The Hebrew word generally rendered *house* might well be able to encompass such notions as a *receptacle, cage* or even *spider's web*. Greek may further split what we lump together as *house* and use two words. Hebrew may have a single word which covers both English *temple* and *palace*. There is no single English equivalent for the Hebrew word sometimes rendered *queen mother* which will convey her status and role in the Israelite royal court. Particularly in the realm of abstractions, it is generally difficult to find one English word which is going to correspond to one Hebrew or Greek word.

Words also take on new meanings and lose old ones over time. *Jealousy* can hardly be used in a good sense in contemporary English, so the phrase *godly jealousy* (used in some translations of 2 Cor 11:2) may strike us as rather odd. The Hebrew word traditionally translated *vanity* (KJV) in Eccl 1:2 hardly covers the current semantic range of this English word. A glance at other translations reveals something of the struggle translators have: *meaningless* (NIV2011, NLT); *emptiness* (NEB); *futile* (NET); *smoke* (Message). My own translation of the expression, *frustrating*, would place it more in the psychological realm, but no one translation may be adequate to encapsulate the meaning.

> What is one lexeme in Hebrew or Greek may take two or more to render in English (and vice versa). There is no such thing as a 'word for word' literal translation.

As you begin to gain facility in the language, you are encouraged to consult more comprehensive lexicons and think about which nuance best fits a particular context rather than slavishly giving the listed gloss as a translation in every context. Better still would be to do your own thorough concordance or electronic search to see some of the points within an imaginary circle of meaning (with fuzzy boundaries) and think creatively about what other possible meanings could fit within that circle (a more useful exercise for words of limited occurrence).

§1.2.3 Grammar in the Narrower Sense

However, this book is not primarily about phonology or semantics, but about the descriptive framework we use for thinking about and discussing how language works. Is there such a thing as a universal grammar? That is, can we lay down a set of 'rules' by which all languages function? At one level, many linguists believe we can usefully set out some principles by which all known natural languages operate. Thus all languages, for example, have nouns and verbs and ways of indicating who the actors in a sentence are and who the targets of an operation are. All languages have words which can further modify these nouns and verbs to increase the subtlety and descriptive power of language. Arguably there are similar processes operating across all languages at a deep level because our brains are similarly wired. But anyone who has studied another language at even a rudimentary level will realise that we quickly face limitations in outlining a general grammar because the particulars of grammatical systems are unique to each language. An older way of teaching English grammar did try to force English to conform to a universal grammar based on Latin, and there are relics of this to be found particularly in textbooks of Greek. This partly works since Latin, Greek and

English do have common origins in the Indo-European family of languages and hence have some grammatical structures in common. However, such an approach is restrictive and forces English into a mould that it should not be made to fit. Hebrew (a Semitic language) is not related to English (except on some fringe theories), so we may expect the particular realisations of its grammatical features to be less familiar to English speakers.

§1.2.3.1 Prescriptive or Descriptive Grammar

Most people who know a little formal grammar learned it or absorbed it in a more or less prescriptivist environment. That is, we have a notion that there is a 'correct' grammar whether or not we are consistent in applying the 'rules' ourselves: 'never split an infinitive'; 'never end a sentence with a preposition', etc. But who says so? The approach of this book is rather to be descriptive and analytical, recognising that there is often more than one acceptable or competent way of saying things and more than one way of analysing what is said.

Further, English is a dynamic language. Not only do we lose old words and gain new ones; we also (more slowly) lose old grammatical 'rules' and gain new ones. To this point I have placed the word 'rules' in quotes to indicate that these are not fixed laws, as though to break them was almost a criminal offence. A **rule** is really an observation of what is generally considered appropriate for a particular mode of communication. It might be better to speak of standard and non-standard modes of expression and to recognise that there are different **registers** or levels of language formality, each with its own rules, such as informal conversation, public address or literary composition. Older grammars told us that we should say: *To whom shall we go?* rather than: *Who will we go to?* and that we should say: *It is she* rather than: *It's her,* but usage (at least in speech and increasingly in writing) does not support these observations and the task of grammar is to describe current usage, not to perpetuate artificial rules or forms from a bygone age. Consider the shift we observe over the twenty or so years (or at least in the chosen register) in the following two translations of Matt 17:25:

From whom do kings of the earth take toll or tribute? (NRSV)
Who do earthly kings collect tariffs or taxes from? (HCSB)

There is room for flexibility in the application of grammatical rules. The apostle Paul, a native Greek speaker, not infrequently breaks rules set out in elementary grammars. We need to keep in mind at all times that language is a means to an end. We do things with words. We seek to inform or to elicit information or to direct. A grammar helps us understand how these objectives of language are accomplished.

Recent decades have seen a lot of developments in **linguistics** (the study of language systems) and the application of the insights gained to English and to the biblical languages, though introductory textbooks on the latter have been slow to pick up on much of this. There are many systems of grammatical description. A grammar will be more or less useful in accordance with its ability to provide a satisfying account of what speakers or writers do when they construct coherent utterances. The approach to grammar adopted here is along fairly traditional lines (as opposed, for example, to a transformational-generative approach), because its aim is to serve as a companion to the elementary grammar textbooks of the biblical languages in particular. However, readers with some knowledge of traditional English grammar might find some of the descriptions different from those they are familiar with. I acknowledge my indebtedness to the more recent grammatical work exemplified in *The Cambridge Grammar of the English Language* (*CGEL*) which to some extent recasts traditional grammatical categories and descriptions (e.g. by greatly expanding the category of prepositions), but I have not adopted every aspect of that descriptive system as not being the most useful for the purpose for which this book is designed.

§1.2.3.2 Morphology and Syntax

Grammar in the narrower sense defined above may be subdivided into two main branches: **morphology** (or **accidence**), which deals with the forms of words and the smallest meaningful elements that make them up, such as **affixes** (prefixes and suffixes), and **syntax**, which deals with the way words are put together in combination to form meaningful sentences.

§1.2.3.2.1 Morphology

Words themselves may be analysed into their components. A word may consist of a **lexical** element (the core of the word with a dictionary meaning) and other elements such as **prefixes** (joined to the beginning of a word) and **suffixes** (joined to the end). The word *unsuspecting* can be broken up into the elements *un-* + *suspect* + *-ing*. The core of the word, its lexical meaning, is contained in the element *suspect* (which has a dictionary meaning), while *un-* and *-ing* serve to specify more precisely the way the word relates to the rest of the sentence.

We have no doubt observed that words take somewhat different forms, depending on their precise meaning or role, though we may not be able to identify why:

Kings <u>run</u> away.

but:

The hired hand <u>runs</u> away.
I have <u>shown</u> you many good deeds.

but:

He <u>showed</u> them his hands and his feet.

English uses **inflected** (marked) forms to a limited extent. A small subclass of words, for example, has different forms depending on whether they function as the subject or the object (§2.3.3). Thus in the sentence:

The rest of the blood <u>he</u> <u>sprinkled</u> against the altar.

we note two inflected forms. English employs a distinct subject or nominative form *he* which makes it clear (despite the atypical word order) that *he* is the one who performed the action of the verb *sprinkled*. The verb *sprinkled* (in contrast, e.g., with *sprinkles*) is an inflected preterite form (§3.7.1.4) most commonly (but not exclusively) used to indicate an action in past time.

As a student of Hebrew or Greek you will become aware that these ancient languages use a considerably larger number of variant forms or **inflections** of a single lexeme and consequently rely a lot more than English on the distinctive forms to indicate grammatical relationships. The simplest lexical form of a word in English is said to be **unmarked** (i.e. has no added morphemes). **Marked** or inflected forms of words have morphemes to indicate such grammatical functions as the plural, the possessive form, a past tense, etc., as well as other modifications such as word-negation (§6.1.1) or feminine gender (§2.3.2).

The exercise of **parsing** a word involves identifying its morphological form and the function it exercises. If asked to parse the word *her* in the following sentence:

He gave <u>her</u> his hand.

we might say that it is a personal pronoun, feminine in gender, singular in number, third person, and that it serves as the indirect object of the verb *gave*. These terms are all explained later.

§1.2.3.2.2 Syntax

Syntax deals with the structure of clauses — how words function in combination. Most readers will be familiar with the traditional classification of words into functional classes or **parts of speech** (nouns, verbs, adjectives, etc.) This classification is helpful as long as we realise that the classification is not determined by some fixed rule based on a word's form but indicates its role in a given context. We sense, for example, that *following* is connected with the verb *follow*. It is in fact a participle (§3.7.3.2.2), retaining its verbal force in:

They have left the straight road, <u>following</u> the road of Balaam.

Yet it is a preposition (as defined at §5.1) in:

<u>*Following*</u> *the flood, Noah lived for 350 years.*

It functions as a noun in:

The <u>following</u> were the sons of Levi …

and as an adjective (§4.2) in:

They came to him the <u>following</u> year.

These are the parts of speech (based on *CGEL*) we will work with: noun, verb, adjective, adverb, preposition, determinative, coordinator, subordinator and interjection.

> Grammars of Hebrew and Greek largely work with similar parts of speech with some minor regrouping. Pronouns (treated here as a subcategory of nouns) might be considered one of the major parts of speech as may the definite article (here grouped with determinatives). Other determinatives might be classed as adjectives. There may be a category of 'particle' which is a loose catch-all for words which can be identified as other parts of speech such as determinative, coordinator, subordinator or interjection. Some prepositions might be classified as conjunctions. The important thing is not the label, but understanding the function.

As well as knowing what a word's job is in itself, we need to know how it is functioning in relation to the words around it — how they affect its meaning and it affects theirs. The mind works by grouping words into meaningful clusters of smaller and larger units, which we call phrases, clauses and sentences. It is understanding the relationship of words to phrases and phrases to clauses and clauses to sentences that enables us to decode a text. We are intuitively aware that certain words are structurally more significant than others. Some words 'depend on' other words. Some words need others to complete their sense.

Some words are not prominent at one level of analysis, but assume a greater prominence at another as we break a sentence down further.

While we mostly do this analysis subconsciously, it will help to be able to talk about this process as we come to learn another language. This broader task we may call **construal**. To construe a sentence involves both parsing of individual words and working out their relationships (partly through word order). After our best efforts there may remain ambiguities of analysis and sometimes these reflect (perhaps at times deliberate) ambiguities in the text. For now one example will suffice:

And all that dwell upon the earth shall worship him, whose names are not written in the book of life of the Lamb slain from the foundation of the world. (Rev 13:8 KJV)

Does *from the foundation of the world* go with *slain* or *written*? Some theological debates hang on such a question. On the whole however, communication works because competent speakers of a language share an understanding of the structural relationships between the elements of a discourse. In the end, context and common sense play their part in interpretation.

§1.2.4 The Basic Units of Language: Some Definitions

§1.2.4.1 The Clause and Its Elements

The minimum requirement for meaningful communication (beyond simply pointing out items, or making a list) is the **clause** consisting of a subject and a predicate (though we will deal later with those clauses where one of these elements is implied rather than stated; §3.3.2.1, §7.1). Loosely speaking, the **subject** (a noun phrase) is the grammatical focus, the person or thing or concept that the clause is saying something about; the **predicate** is what is being said about it, typically including a verb to indicate some action performed, or state experienced, or relationship sustained by the subject. The shortest verse in the KJV, John 11:35, illustrates this:

Jesus wept.

Here the sentence consists of just one clause with one word, *Jesus*, in the subject slot + one word, the verb *wept*, in the predicate slot. We may call the verb (as **head** of the predicate) the **predicator**. We do find some verbless clauses in English, particularly in short exclamations and proverbial expressions, though we sense these to be incomplete grammatically:

No wonder!
Like mother, like daughter.

By definition a clause contains only one verb (or implied verb), bearing in mind that a verb, as we will define it, may consist of more than one word:

The Lord <u>has been speaking</u> to me.

This is still one clause, with one predicate consisting of one compound verb *has been speaking* (§3.4).

The verb may be finite (§3.7.3.1), in which case the clause is finite and capable of functioning as an independent clause; or the verb may be non-finite (§3.7.3.2), in which case the clause is non-finite and can only function as an embedded or subordinate clause (§7.2). Older grammars did not recognise non-finite clauses, preferring to call them phrases.

Most utterances include other elements, whether in the subject slot or the predicate slot. These added elements fall into two broad categories: **modifiers** which serve to further identify, describe or nuance other constituents in some way and **complements** which add to, or fill out other constituents. Consider the sentence:

Impatient people do foolish things.

We sense that the words *impatient people* belong together as who it is that is being spoken about, while the rest of the sentence says something about or predicates something of them. The predicator is *do*. But *do* by itself tells us very little about the subject's activity. It has going closely with it an expression that completes or fills out or complements what it is that impatient people *do*, namely *foolish things*. *Foolish things* is then a **complement** of the verb (to be more specific its direct object). We could further analyse the subject into its head word *people* + a modifier (here an adjective) *impatient*. Similarly the object *foolish things* could be broken down into a modifier (to be more precise an adjective) *foolish* + a noun *things* (the head word of its noun phrase). Thus we might usefully speak of **head words** and optional modifiers and complements. What is a complement at one level may then consist of a head word at a lower level of the hierarchy and itself take a modifier or complement. We may diagram the sentence above as follows:

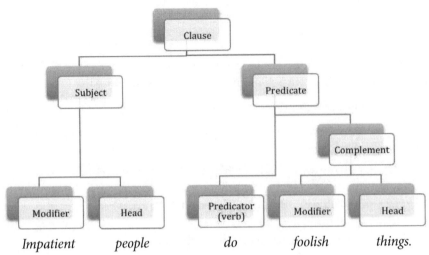

While not every grammatical descriptive system works on the principle of a hierarchy of branching (particularly binary) elements, this tree diagramming system can be a helpful tool for analysis. Words belong more closely with some elements in the sentence than with others and (though we may rarely picture a tree diagram as we speak or write or listen or read) we do somehow keep together mentally those elements that are intended to go with each other in the task of construing the sentence.

Languages differ in how they indicate these grammatical relationships. While English has some marked or inflectional forms as noted above, it relies significantly on word order. We intuitively recognise that normally when a noun comes before a verb in a declarative sentence it suggests that that noun is doing that verb, i.e. it is the subject of the clause. In the sentence:

God created the heavens.

we have no difficulty understanding who created what, even though there are no grammatical markers for subject or object here. There are variations to this typical pattern, but competent speakers generally have little difficulty in discerning the connections and relationships of words. See §2.3.3.1 and §3.1 for more on recognition of subjects and verbs.

In inflected languages (like Hebrew and Greek), where the pronoun subject is identified in the verb form, finite clauses (those containing a subject and a verb in a particular tense) are frequently expressed with a single word form: *she-gave*; *they-fall*.

§1.2.4.1.1 Canonical Clauses

It will also be helpful to recognise that the basic thing we do with words is make declarations about reality (or our perception of it). The other things we do (ask questions, make denials, express desires, etc.) can be considered as **transformations** of the basic declarative sentence. The word **canonical** is used in grammar for such basic declarations (though biblical students need to be aware that this has nothing to do with the canon of Scripture!). Thus, a passive clause, for example (§3.7.2.2), is a transformation of a canonical active clause. A negative clause is a transformation of a canonical positive clause. A question is a transformation of a canonical affirmation.

§1.2.4.2 The Phrase

A **phrase** is the next smaller unit than the clause. A phrase is strictly any combination of head word ± complement or modifier (i.e. a phrase on this definition may consist of a single word since the complement or modifier is optional) functioning as a single constituent unit within a clause. In practice, we can often skip the phrase level of analysis and refer to the subject of a clause as a noun rather than a noun phrase consisting of a head word (a noun) with or without adjuncts. A particular phrase type is the prepositional phrase: *in the beginning; for all eternity; within the palace*, which will be dealt with at §5.1.3.

§1.2.4.3 The Sentence

At a higher level than the clause stands the **sentence**. While a sentence may consist of a single clause, most English sentences in written texts consist of two or more clauses. Clauses may be linked in parallel (coordinated) or arranged in a theoretically infinite hierarchy (though there are clearly practical limits!) of embedded or subordinate clauses nested within one another. These will be dealt with in Chapter 7.

We turn next to consider one of the fundamental units of language, the noun.

Exercises for Chapter 1

1. Is there a phonemic difference between the *s* sound in *sure* and the *s* sound in *son*?

2. Group the following words according to their lexemes: *sizes, larger, enlarge, biggest, large, size, enlarging.* (Hint: one of the lexemes needed is not in the list!)

3. Break the following words into their morphemes: *puts, foolishness, disagreement, unreasonable, illnesses.*

4. True or False: A word's part of speech can be determined by its morphology, e.g. a word ending in *-ing* is a verb form.

5. Identify the subjects and predicates in the following clauses:
    a. *We ought to love one another.*
    b. *I and all the people who are with me will approach the city.*
    c. *The women of the neighbourhood gave him a name.*
    d. *Never again will there be a flood.*

2. Nouns by the Case

Nouns are the participants of discourse in any language. A noun (as defined below) is an essential element in every clause either expressly or, in the case of directive clauses (§3.7.3.1.4) and with ellipsis or gapping (§7.1), implied. Nouns identify the persons speaking or addressed and the characters or items under discussion. Either alone or in combination with determinatives, adjectives or other modifiers (including longer phrases and clauses), nouns fill the slot of noun phrases in the constituent structure of a clause (§1.2.4.1).

Typically nouns refer to persons or items we can see or otherwise experience through our senses. More broadly they provide labels to help us identify individual members of a class, or to group and identify categories of persons, living things, objects, events, or concepts in our experience (including our imagination), relate them to similar experiences and distinguish them from different ones.

The use of a noun in a particular context may refer in principle to the whole class, or to any typical member of the class, or to a specific instance of the item. The nouns in the following sentences are underlined:

The _camel_ is unclean.
Do not take _advantage_ of a _widow_ or an _orphan_.
The next _day_ the _wind_ came up.
There were some _men_ from _Cyprus_ and _Cyrene_.
Put on the new _man_ created in _God's_ _image_, in _righteousness_ and _holiness_.

§2.1 Types of Noun

Nouns may be classified according to several types: common nouns, proper nouns and pronouns, with further subdivisions of these.

§2.1.1 Common Nouns

Common nouns are those that refer typically to non-unique members of classes of people, places, things, events, concepts, etc. We could distinguish between those common nouns that are more **concrete** (*earth, music, aroma*), because more immediately perceived by the senses, and those which are more **abstract** (*fearfulness, maturity, redemption*), though this distinction is more semantic than grammatical and there is a spectrum ranging from concrete to abstract. The more abstract nouns may be a little harder to recognise as nouns, as we do not experience them in the same direct and sensory way as common nouns.

§2.1.2 Proper Nouns

Nouns (or perhaps more strictly in some cases noun phrases) which identify a particular person by name or title, or a particular place, particular literary or artistic creation (such as a book), a unique event, festival, day, month, people group, society, movement, or sometimes their individual members, are called **proper nouns**, distinguished in English (and for some of the above categories in Greek) by being capitalised: *God* (conventionally capitalised in distinction from *god* for the God of the Bible), the *Holy Spirit*, my *Rock*, *Caesar Augustus*, *Galilee*, the *Reed Sea*, the *Book of the Wars of the Lord*, the *Sadducees*, a *Nazirite*, *Judaism*, the *Sabbath*, the month *Nisan*. Of course there can be more than one *Judas* or *Caesarea* but in context the name will generally have a unique referent. Proper nouns are inherently definite whether or not they have a determinative such as the definite article (§4.1.3).

§2.1.3 Pronouns

Pronouns, treated here as a subcategory of nouns, do not of themselves denote any particular persons or things. Their referent is determined by the context. As **pro-forms**, they are placeholders in the constituent structure for other nouns. Pronouns include such words as: *me, they, himself, ours, these, whoever, no-one*. Pronouns differ from most other nouns in that they generally do not accept adjectives in the attributive position (§4.2.7.1), i.e. it is non-standard to say **righteous they* or **unhappy she*.

Some English pronouns have distinctive inflected forms to mark number, gender and case (§2.3). It will be expedient, then, to defer a more detailed consideration of the types and functions of pronouns till after a treatment of the properties of nouns (see §2.4).

§2.2 Noun Formation

The majority of English nouns have no formal features to identify them as nouns. Nouns can be identical in form to or 'borrowed' from other word categories. Many adjectives, for example, can readily be used substantivally as nouns (§4.2.8).

English words can often without change be either a verb or a noun. Words like *love, hope, desire, walk, wonder, cook, sacrifice* are verbs in some situations, and nouns in others. Some nouns, besides being derived from or related to verbs, retain some verbal characteristics. These will be dealt elsewhere under verbal nouns (§3.7.3.2.1). Some words which were originally verbal nouns have lost much of their verbal force and are simply treated as nouns: *a burnt offering*; *the meaning of this*; *a nation with no understanding*; *a wise saying*; *a dwelling for demons*.

> Hebrew and Greek, like English, often use closely related forms for nouns and verbs in the same semantic area, though the formal features of nouns and particularly verbs in these languages mean that for the most part the verb form will be distinguishable from the related noun form by its ending or other inflectional element.

Some nouns do have distinctive suffixes (§1.2.3.2.1) which help to identify particular classes of noun. Many nouns ending in *-er* have a similar function: *builder, maker, teacher, healer*. All these identify the person who does the job identified in the verbs *build, make, teach, heal*. They may be called **agent nouns**. Words which end in *-ship* such as *lordship, kingship, friendship* are used for the abstract quality connected with the role of a *lord*, or *king* or *friend*. The ending *-ion* often marks nouns indicating the process or result of an action: *confusion, consecration, contribution, situation*. The suffix *-ness*, typically added to adjectives, creates a noun denoting the quality or state associated with the adjective: *nakedness, darkness, kindness, holiness, brightness*. An *-ism* (actually a Greek morpheme which English has borrowed) often refers to a movement or ideology: *Pharisaism, Judaism*.

> Hebrew and Greek similarly have some noun classes with characteristic formal features.

Nouns can also be compounded from two or more other words, particularly other shorter nouns. Thus in English we have *leatherworker*, *bodyguard* and *craftsman*.

> Hebrew only uses this means of noun-formation to a very limited extent (e.g. the valley of *death-shadow* in Ps 23:4), but Greek uses it quite frequently (e.g. words for *God-lover, evildoer, foolish talk*).

§2.3 Characteristics of Nouns

Nouns possess a number of characteristics such as number and case, some of which are inflectionally marked (§1.2.3.2.1), some of which are determined by word order and context. The listing of the different forms and functions a noun may have is known as a **declension**. To analyse a noun in terms of its particular characteristics and function (such as number and case) is to **decline** it.

§2.3.1 Number

Nouns can be countable or essentially non-countable. Countable nouns can occur in the **singular number** (the unmarked form) when only one item is envisaged or the class as a whole (*The camel is unclean*). When more than one item is in view, the plural form is used. The **plural** of nouns is typically marked by adding -*(e)s* (with possible slight spelling adjustment): *boys, witnesses, cities*. A few nouns form their plurals in other ways: *men, women, children, feet, teeth, oxen*. A few nouns experience no change in the plural: *sheep, deer, fish*. For words borrowed from other languages, English sometimes used the foreign plural forms, though the use of these foreign plurals is in decline: *cherubim, seraphim, Urim* and *Thummim* (Hebrew plural forms); *denarii* (Latin plural form); *Magi* (a Latinised Greek plural). For plurals of personal pronouns and associated emphatic and reflexive forms, see §2.4.

A **collective** noun (a subcategory of common nouns) is one that refers to a group or collection of individual persons, living things or other items, such as *herd, crowd, people, assembly* (whether or not viewed as physically in one place at the time). Collective nouns may be treated as either singular or plural and even switch from one to the other in a single sentence, depending on whether the group is considered more as a single entity, or an aggregation of individuals:

The people are foolish. (plural)
I have seen this people (singular)*, and they are* (plural) *a stiff-necked people* (singular) *indeed!*
A crowd was sitting around him (singular).
A large crowd were leaving Jericho (plural).

Abstract nouns are not normally countable, but can be pluralised particularly in the sense of *instances of …* or *types of …*:

They did not remember your many kindnesses.
Avoid the gossip and absurdities of so-called knowledge.

While English does not really possess the **dual** as a grammatical category, words like *pair, both, couple* could be considered inherently dual. Somewhat analogous also are the plural forms which lack a singular (of the same sense of the word) because they belong in a bipartite structure: *scales, shears*. Hebrew has a distinct inflectional form for the dual used mainly for things which naturally occur in pairs such as *eyes, hands, feet*.

§2.3.2 Gender

English speakers may not be familiar with **gender** as a grammatical category apart from the natural division of words according to the biological sex of the items represented: *boy, uncle* (masculine); *queen, cow* (feminine); *rock, nothing* (neuter). For some words, a gendered pair of **masculine** and **feminine** words exists, such as for animals and some occupation terms: *lion : lioness; master : mistress; prophet : prophetess* though the feminine forms of some such words are on the way out in favour of gender-neutral terms. Occasionally we personify items such as ships or cities or countries and treat them as feminine:

Egypt and <u>her</u> gods.
Speak tenderly to Jerusalem, and cry to <u>her</u> …

Apart from this, we regard as **neuter** gender (neither masculine or feminine) all nouns referring to non-animate entities (and even those representing animals where sex is not a feature of the discussion). English uses distinct masculine, feminine and neuter singular personal pronouns (he, she, it) to refer to these largely natural genders.

Many languages have a grammatical gender in which all nouns are classed as masculine or feminine (so Hebrew, French), or as masculine, feminine or neuter (so Greek, German). Even where a neuter category exists, many words without biological gender may belong in the masculine or feminine category.

There is no point in trying to psychologise the language to discover why a word for *love* might be considered feminine, for example, or a word for *time* masculine. It is going to be important to learn the gender of each new noun you learn for the relevant gendered pronoun form will normally be used to refer to it, as well as any adjectives and possibly determinatives. In Hebrew even some verb forms are gender marked and so must conform to the gender of the noun. One feature, true for both Hebrew and Greek, is that the masculine is the default form, and (unlike modern English) speakers were comfortable using a masculine collective or plural form to include both genders. So the plural of the word for *brother* in Greek is often best rendered *brothers and sisters*. Where a particular grammatical form is unmarked for gender (i.e. can refer to either masculine or feminine) the term **common** is used. Thus first person pronoun forms (e.g. *I, me, we, us*) in English (as in Hebrew and Greek) are always common gender.

§2.3.3 Case

As nouns exercise different functions (in subject or non-subject roles) in the clause structure, they may be said to possess the property of **case**. In

English, the case of a noun is largely unmarked inflectionally, and determined by word order or other contextual considerations. Note how the following sentences have different meanings, though they contain precisely the same elements:

God loves the world.
The world loves God.

However, some pronoun forms (§2.4) are marked for case, so English speakers can observe the distinctions between case forms in operation. English also marks its genitive case for all nouns (§2.3.3.2.2).

> While Hebrew and Greek have patterns and preferences in word order, they are not so dependent on word order for identifying the case function of nouns. Greek generally distinguishes the case of nouns (including pronouns) by an inflection. Hebrew does not mark cases as such for nouns, but does commonly use a marker for nouns used as direct objects when these are definite.

§2.3.3.1 Nominative or Subjective Case

The **nominative case** is typically the case of the subject of a finite clause, the noun which performs the action, or experiences the state referred to in the verb, or is the focus of a verbless clause. The subject in English is inflectionally unmarked (apart from distinctive nominative forms for some pronouns) and typically comes before its verb in affirmative declarations. The subject might come later in the clause under some circumstances, e.g. in questions or when the object or some other constituent is fronted for highlighting (and pronoun inflections may help to distinguish subject and object). To find the subject of a verb, first find the verb (§3.1), then ask 'who?' or 'what?' + verb, making sure to keep all the elements of a compound verb (§3.4) together. So in the clause:

To you has been given the secret of the kingdom.

ask:

What has been given? (not: *Who gave?*)
King Xerxes was feeling the effects of the wine.
Never again will there be a flood to destroy the earth.
These things you have done.
To the only wise God be glory and honour.

In some sentences, particularly directives (commands), the subject may not be expressed:

Give her to me.

The implied subject of *give* is the addressee as in all direct commands, i.e. *you*.

Nouns having the same referent as the subject may be joined with the subject in the grammatical relationship of **apposition**, and are in the nominative case:

We — the priests, the Levites and the people — have cast lots.
His son Ishmael was thirteen.

Another use of the nominative is for the **predicative** complement of a verb of *being* or *becoming*, i.e. the noun following equative verbs. While the accusative (objective) case may be used in the predicate slot in more contemporary speech, the nominative is still the preferred literary form:

You were strangers.
It is I.

The focus of verbless clauses, as well as simple lists, vocabularies, dictionary entries, epistolary formulas and headings that do not constitute clauses are given in the nominative case:

Every man to his tent, O Israel! (verbless clause)
Grace and peace to you from God our Father and the Lord Jesus Christ.
Revelation.

§2.3.3.2 Oblique Cases

Nouns may also occur in a range of other relationships to the clause, including direct and indirect objects, possessives, and the complements of prepositional phrases. While English employs limited inflectional marking for such **oblique cases** as they are called, possessives are marked in all nouns and there is an inflectional form different from the nominative for some pronouns.

§2.3.3.2.1 Accusative Case or Direct Object Case

The **accusative** or **objective case** is the case used typically for the **direct object**, i.e. the item directly acted upon in the verb. While English has no inflected form to mark the accusative case of most nouns, some pronouns have an oblique case used (among other functions) for the direct object (*me, him, her, us, them*). A direct object usually comes after its verb in English, though this word order may be varied e.g. by fronting of the object in order to highlight it. Observe the direct objects in the following sentences:

Pilate washed his hands.
They crucified the Lord of glory.

Remember the Sabbath <u>day</u>.
<u>Silver</u> and <u>gold</u> have I none. (The object is fronted.)
<u>Jesus</u> I know, and <u>Paul</u> I know; but who are you? (The objects are fronted.)

A word in the accusative case, while serving as the object of its clause, may also function as the subject of some embedded or dependent non-finite clauses (§7.2).

The master ordered <u>him</u> to be sold.
Have <u>them</u> bring charges.

Accusatives may also occur in apposition (§2.3.3.1) with other accusatives.

§2.3.3.2.2 Genitive or Possessive Case

English has an inflected form for the **possessive** or **genitive case** marked by the addition of -'s or (for some words and names ending in -s and for plural nouns) simply by adding the apostrophe punctuation mark ('). The inflected genitive is (apart from the punctuation which is an attempt to create the appearance of a difference) the same morpheme generally used to indicate the plural — languages have a habit of using a limited number of morphemes for a variety of functions.

In many instances the inflectionally marked genitive with -'s is the equivalent of a prepositional phrase with *of* + the unmarked form of the noun, though *of* expressions can more readily convey a wider range of relationships than the inflected genitive. The form with *of* is used in preference to a chain of inflected genitives. While typically marking possession, authorship, kinship and the like, something of the range of relationships that can be expressed by the genitive form is indicated in the following examples:

The <u>man's</u> wife.
The earth is the <u>Lord's</u>.
They found the man sitting at <u>Jesus'</u> feet.
Even the dogs eat the crumbs that fall from their <u>master's</u> table.
Your <u>children's</u> children.
Do to Ai and <u>its</u> king what you did to Jericho and <u>its</u> king.
This perfume could have been sold for well over a <u>year's</u> wages.

§2.3.3.2.2.1 Subjective and Objective Genitive

Two important uses of the genitive are the **subjective** and the **objective genitive**. These terms are applicable only to genitives going closely with other nouns with some verbal force. To identify a subjective genitive, ask *who* or *what* would be the subject of the verbal idea in the accompanying noun. If the answer is the person or thing in the genitive word, it is a subjective genitive:

This is your doing.
The sound of the people's weeping.
Their testimony was not the same.
By one man's obedience many will be made righteous.

To identify an objective genitive, ask *who* or *what* would be the object of the verbal idea in the accompanying noun. If the answer is the person or thing in the genitive word, it is an objective genitive:

The priests' anointing is to admit them to a perpetual priesthood.
There is one body and one Spirit, just as you were called to the one hope of your calling.
Who has known the mind of God or who has become his counsellor?

Of course only context can distinguish these, and ambiguities will remain. Consider the following:

The love of Christ compels us (as in 2 Cor 5:14). Does this mean *the love Christ has for us* (subjective) or *the love we have for Christ* (objective)? You can't tell without more information, and there is a lot of discussion and disagreement amongst commentators at times over phrases like this. Generally translations will attempt to disambiguate (according to their understanding) by means of such phrases as *love for Christ* if they understand it as objective. We should be open to the possibility that both subjective and objective may be intended in some contexts.

§2.3.3.2.2.2 Predicative Genitive

The **predicative genitive** is used in the predicate position (§1.2.4.1), i.e. without further accompanying noun. There are distinctive inflectional forms for a number of the personal pronouns in this case function in English:

The earth is the Lord's.
All that you see is mine.
Blessed are those who are persecuted for righteousness' sake, for theirs is the kingdom of heaven.
She mistreats her young as if they were not hers.
Let's kill him so the inheritance will be ours.

§2.3.3.2.3 Dative Case or Indirect Object Case

The **indirect object** is typically the person or item indirectly affected by the action of the verb, or who has an interest in the action, such as benefiting from it. In English it is often the equivalent of a phrase introduced by the prepositions *to* or *for*, though in some constructions, typically after verbs such as *give, send, tell, write, make* the noun (including pronouns) may be without preposition if coming between the verb and the direct object and this form is sometimes called the **dative case** (though inflectionally indistinguishable from the accusative case in English):

Come, make <u>us</u> gods.
Moses wrote <u>you</u> this law.
Solomon gave <u>her</u> more than she had brought him.

Note how this *her* is functionally different from the direct object *her* in:

Sarai took Hagar and gave <u>her</u> to her husband.

Note the indirect object is not the same as a second direct object possible with some verbs. Thus the sentence above *Come, make us gods* (Exod 32:1) is functionally equivalent to *Come, make gods for us*, whereas *Make us slaves* (Gen 43:18) means *Make us (become) slaves.*

> Hebrew typically uses an equivalent to English *to* for indirect objects, while Greek uses the dative case.

§2.3.3.2.4 Case of Prepositional Complements

English is generally said to use the accusative case for the noun following a preposition, though we are calling this the **prepositional complement** rather than (with older grammars) the 'object' of the preposition:

In <u>the beginning</u>, God created the heavens and the earth.
Hasn't he also spoken through <u>us</u>?
The ground that was under <u>them</u> split open.
The name of <u>the man</u> with <u>whom</u> I worked today is Boaz.

> Greek employs all of its oblique cases for prepositional complements, sometimes all three with the same preposition used in different senses.

§2.3.3.2.5 Vocative Case

The **vocative case** is the form we use to address someone (or something) by name or by some other word (such as a title). The word in the vocative is an element often not closely tied to the remainder of the clause structure. The vocative is often omitted for the sake of simplicity in listings of case forms and is not always included in the definition of an oblique case as discussed above. There is no distinctive inflectional form in English for the vocative case. In Greek a distinctive form does exist for some nouns, while others simply use the nominative. The one Greek vocative form which has carried across into English in some old hymns is the form *Jesu*. Vocatives may be preceded in English by the determinative *O*. Consider the following vocatives:

O king, live forever.
Saul, Saul, why do you persecute me?

In these cases, the vocatives have the same referent as the subject (or implied subject) of the verb, and so might be confused with the subject. The vocative word may also have the same referent as a word in another constituent slot, e.g. direct object:

Lord, why can't I follow you now?

or indirect object:

Let all the kings of the earth give you thanks, O Lord.

In the following sentences, the vocatives are grammatically unrelated to the subject or any other noun in the clause:

Lord, how can I know that I will gain possession of it?
Every man to his tent, O Israel!

Inanimate objects may also occasionally be addressed in the vocative, in which case we call the literary device **apostrophe**.

Altar, altar! This is what the Lord says.
O Jerusalem, Jerusalem, you who kill the prophets and stone those who are sent to you!

§2.4 Types of Pronoun

Pronouns are of a number of types which we could categorise as personal, deictic, emphatic, reflexive, interrogative, relative, indefinite, negative and reciprocal.

§2.4.1 Personal Pronouns

The personal pronouns are *I* (with oblique case forms: *me, my, mine*); *you* (*your, yours*); *he* (*him, his*); *she* (*her, hers*); *it* (*its*); *we* (*our, ours*); *they* (*them, their, theirs*). These stand as substitutes for identifiable persons or things, either as **anaphora** (picking up a more explicit mention elsewhere in the context of the utterance), or **deixis** (pointing out someone or something):

The man knew <u>his</u> wife Eve, and <u>she</u> conceived (anaphora; *his* substitutes for *the man's* and *she* substitutes for *his wife*).
Who is <u>he</u> walking in the field? (deixis).

> Hebrew and Greek each have a set of personal pronouns functioning in much the same way as English, though having verb forms inflected for person, pronouns are needed less frequently than in English.

§2.4.1.1 The Person in Personal Pronouns

Personal pronouns, besides having distinctive number, gender and case, are also marked for **person**. We speak of potentially three persons within discourse. The speaker, alone (*I, me, my, mine*) or with any others the speaker identifies with and includes in a *we* (*us, our, ours*) reference, is the **first person**:

O Lord <u>my</u> God, <u>I</u> called to you for aid and you healed <u>me</u>.
If <u>we</u> confess <u>our</u> sins, he is faithful and just and will forgive <u>us</u> <u>our</u> sins.

> There is a logical difference between the **exclusive** and **inclusive** *we* depending on whether the person(s) addressed are also included; however, English (along with Hebrew and Greek) does not distinguish these in any formal way:

How is it that <u>we</u> and the Pharisees fast often, but your disciples do not fast? (exclusive)
<u>We</u> all stumble in many ways. (inclusive)

The person or persons addressed are called the **second person**, *you* (*your, yours*):

<u>You</u> will crawl on <u>your</u> belly.
Any children that <u>you</u> father after them will be <u>yours</u>.

Anyone or anything else is a third party in the discourse, or, grammatically speaking, in the **third person**. The relevant third person personal pronoun forms are *he* (*him, his*), *she* (*her, hers*), *it* (*its*), *they* (*them, their, theirs*):

If <u>she</u> does separate, let <u>her</u> remain unmarried.
<u>He</u> measured <u>its</u> wall.
The second death has no power over <u>them</u>, but <u>they</u> will be priests of God.

I, he, she, it (with their other cases) are singular. *You* (with its other cases) is either singular or plural. *They* (with its other cases) is traditionally plural. However *they* is increasingly used as a singular because it is gender-neutral:

If anyone thinks <u>they</u> are something when <u>they</u> are not, <u>they</u> deceive <u>themselves</u>. (Gal 6:3 NIV2011)

Much or what is said above in relation to person, number and case of personal pronouns applies also to those pronoun forms based on personal pronouns (emphatic: §2.4.3; reflexive: §2.4.4).

§2.4.2 Deictic or Demonstrative Pronouns

There is considerable conceptual overlap between **deictic** (or **demonstrative**) **pronouns** (*this, that, these, those*) and the deictic use of third person personal pronouns. *He* (when used deictically to point out a male person) is little different from *that (man)* and translations may render the same Hebrew or Greek expressions in either of these ways:

<u>These</u> *were the heroes that were of old.* (Gen 6:4 NRSV)
<u>They</u> *were the heroes of old.* (Gen 6:4 NIV2011)

Deictics point out someone or something, either literally (perhaps with an accompanying gesture) or simply because speaker and hearers are together at a particular place and time:

Who are <u>these</u> with you?
I am pregnant by the man who owns <u>these</u>.
Tell me, is <u>this</u> the price you and Ananias received for the land?' 'Yes,' she replied, '<u>that's</u> the price.'
<u>This</u> *is the day the Lord has made.*

The deixis may relate to the discourse context, not the physical context:

<u>These</u> *are the true words of God* (i.e. the words just given).
<u>This</u> *is the meaning of the parable* (i.e. the explanation about to be given).

English deictics may be **proximal**, i.e. those that refer to closer items (*this, these*), or **distal**, those that refer to more remote items (*that, those*). Of course what is near and what is remote is relative to the situation. Greek reflects these distinctions. Traditionally it was thought that Hebrew did as well, but recent work has cast doubt on this.

Be aware that *this, these, those* and especially *that* have other functions.

§2.4.3 Emphatic Pronouns

Emphatic pronouns highlight other nouns (including pronouns). Emphatics can relate to nouns in any constituent position (subject and non-subject). For most cases, the emphatics are based on a form of the personal pronoun + -*self* (for singular) or -*selves* (for plural):

I myself will go surety for him.
Is it a time for you yourselves to be living in your panelled houses?
The circumcised do not obey the law themselves.

Occasionally an emphatic pronoun can be used alone, without another noun, particularly with directives (commands):

Stop here yourself for a while.

Emphatic pronouns have the same form regardless of whether they emphasise a subject or non-subject case. However, though not generally treated at this point in grammars, there is also a set of genitive emphatic pronoun forms. These differ from the -*self* set, adding instead the word *own* after the genitive forms of the personal pronouns. These forms are sometimes useful in avoiding possible ambiguity:

I will deliver you from your own people.
In the same way, husbands should love their wives as they do their own bodies.

> Hebrew and Greek treat emphatics and reflexives differently. In both languages, the personal pronoun when used with a verb inflected for person (§3.7.3.1.1) may be understood as emphatic.

§2.4.4 Reflexive Pronouns

Reflexive pronouns are used for the direct or indirect object or prepositional complement when this has the same referent as the subject. In English the form of the reflexive pronoun is identical with the emphatic pronoun (-*self*, -*selves*) discussed above (§2.4.3), so it is important to distinguish the different functions they have:

If we say that we have no sin, we are deceiving ourselves.
The sparrow has found herself a home.

§2.4.5 Interrogative Pronouns

An **interrogative pronoun** (*who, whom, what*) introduces a question where the speaker lacks (or purports to lack) an element of information. English uses *who* (*whom*) for persons and *what* for non-persons or where the answer expected is not in terms of personal identity, but of characteristic.

Who are you?
What then is Apollos? What is Paul? Servants through whom you came to believe.
What are you doing here?
To whom shall we go? (literary use)
Who will we go to? (more common in speech)

The word *whose* is a genitive case form of the interrogative pronoun (as though it were a variant spelling of the unused form **who's*):

Whose is this image and superscription?

Because forms of *who* and *which* are also used as relative pronouns (§2.4.6), it is important to be able to distinguish between the interrogative function and the relative function of these words.

> Hebrew and Greek both have a set of interrogative pronouns different from their relative pronouns.

§2.4.6 Relative Pronouns

A **relative pronoun** may be used to link a noun (or noun phrase) in one clause to the same referent (expressed or implied) in another clause. Relative pronouns are *who* (*whom, whose*), *which, whoever, whatever* and *that*. The noun to which the relative pronoun refers is called the **antecedent**. The clause introduced by the relative pronoun is called a relative clause and will be dealt with at §7.2.2.

For now, note that though these relative forms are identical in English with the interrogative pronouns above, they serve a very different function:

These are the kings who reigned in the land of Edom.
This is for the man whom the king chooses to honour.
Write down all these things that have happened to you.
The people to whom they are prophesying will die.

§2.4.7 Indefinite Pronouns

As the name implies, an **indefinite pronoun** expresses an element of generality or vagueness. Indefinite pronouns include *someone, anyone, somebody, anybody, something, whoever, whatever*:

Someone drew a bow by chance and shot the king.
I will give a reward to anyone who enters the city.
Do with her whatever you think best.

Unlike most pronouns, an indefinite pronoun is capable of taking an attributive adjective, in which case the adjective follows the pronoun:

Can anything good come from there?
People swear by someone greater than themselves.

§2.4.8 Negative Pronouns

A **negative pronoun** is effectively a negated indefinite pronoun, indicating the non-existence of a person or thing in the category under consideration. As negatives, they are subject to the rules for negation (§6.1):

Make sure that nobody pays back wrong for wrong.
Nothing was missing.

§2.4.9 Reciprocal Pronouns

A **reciprocal pronoun** is used where each member of a pair or group acts as both subject and an oblique (non-subject) case. Reciprocal pronouns are *one another* and *each other*:

They were calling to one another, 'Holy, holy, holy is the Lord Almighty.'
Greet each other with a holy kiss.

Sometimes, as in the examples above, the mutuality is regarded as exhaustive as each member of the group is envisaged as dealing with each other member of the group in the manner identified. At other times, it is logically a partial reciprocation, where only some members deal with some members:

The people slaughtered each other.
He joined five of the curtains to one another.

Exercises for Chapter 2

1. Identify the nouns (including pronouns) in the following:
   a. *No work is to be done on the seventh day.*
   b. *She prepared some tasty food, the kind he loved.*

    c. *God chose people from the beginning for salvation through sanctification by the Spirit and faith in the truth.*

    d. *One of the disciples was at the table to the right of Jesus in a place of honour.*

    e. *I will surely give you back a tenth of everything you give me.*

2. Identify the pronouns in the following and indicate their type:

    a. *We have never seen anything like this!*

    b. *No-one who seeks to make a reputation for himself does anything in secret.*

    c. *Whom will I send? Who will go for us?*

    d. *By what can I know that I am to possess it?*

    e. *This is how it will be with whoever stores up things for themselves but is not rich toward God.* (Luke 12:21 NIV2011)

3. Identify the direct and indirect objects in the following:

    a. *The Lord will relent from his fierce anger and show you compassion.*

    b. *You will not find me.*

    c. *They heard the voice but saw no-one.*

    d. *He was given authority over every tribe, people, language, and nation.*

    e. *His mother used to make him a small robe.*

    f. *The best of the flocks and cattle they spared to sacrifice to the Lord.*

4. Which of the following underlined words are subjective genitives?

    a. *The <u>children's</u> teeth are set on edge.*

    b. *<u>My</u> punishment is greater than I can bear.*

    c. *<u>Your</u> faith has made you well.*

    d. *Save us, O God of <u>our</u> salvation.*

    e. *This was the <u>Lord's</u> doing.*

5. Identify the relative pronouns in the following and indicate their antecedent:

    a. *They came to a place called Golgotha (which means 'Place of the Skull').*

    b. *These things happened to them as examples and were written for our instruction, on whom the ends of the ages have come.*

    c. *Lift up your eyes on high and see: who created these?*

    d. *Take note of Jesus, the apostle and high priest whom we confess.*

    e. *God saw that the light was good.*

6. Identify the reflexive pronouns in the following:

   a. *Her virgins have been afflicted, and she herself suffers.*

   b. *With the merciful you show yourself merciful.*

   c. *So shall your judgment be; you yourself have decided it.*

   d. *Those who fail to find me harm themselves.*

   e. *To those under the law I became as one under the law (though not being under the law myself).*

3. What Can Verbs Do?

§3.1 What Is a Verb?

The school definition of a **verb** as a 'doing word' is only partially correct, as verbs do more than denote actions. A verb may also signal the existence of a state or a relationship, so a more comprehensive definition might be: A verb indicates what it is that the actors in a sentence *do*, or the *states* in which they exist or the *relationships* they sustain. To be a bit more technical, in a binary division of a clause into subject (the person or thing under discussion) and predicate (what is said about the person or thing), the verb is the head of the predicate, or **predicator**.

We may feel we need little help with identifying verbs that express activity:

God <u>created</u> the heavens and the earth.
I <u>give</u> you a new commandment.

But don't think that the most action-packed looking word is always going to be the verb. Where is the verb in the following sentence?

The race is not to the swift nor the battle to the strong.

It would be wrong to identify *race* or *swift* or *battle* as verbs just because they seem to be 'moving faster' than other words. The only verb in this sentence is *is*! Consider the state or relationship expressed in the following:

The authorities that <u>exist</u> have been established by God.
He <u>was</u> the son of a widow.
Salvation <u>belongs</u> to our God.

To help identify many verbs, first ask yourself if what you think is a verb form (by the criteria given above) is a simple form (or bare form: §3.7.1.1), or can be expressed as a simple form. The simple form is the form used, for example, in issuing directives (commands), or the form of the verb that would be supplied after the expression *I want you to ...* Then, as a check, ask if it would make any sense to add the suffix *-ing* (the gerund-participle form: §3.7.1.3) to the simple form of the verb (perhaps with some minor spelling modification). The simple form of *changed* would be *change* (we can direct someone: *Change!*). *Changing* is also an acceptable form, so *changed* is likely to be a verb form. This works for the vast majority of verbs (but see the discussion of auxiliary verbs: §3.3.2).

39

§3.2 Verb Formation

Verbs can be formed in a variety of ways and many English verbs are identical in form to other parts of speech, so we need to be careful to determine the function of each word in a given context. We need not attempt to discern 'which came first' (like the proverbial chicken and the egg) — the verb or some other function. It does not really matter, for example, whether *love* as a verb is derived from *love* as a noun or the other way around. There is a fallacy which persists in the minds of some students of biblical languages that in Greek and particularly Hebrew 'everything derives from the verb'. Having said that, there is a class of verbs called **denominative** verbs, where the verb is more clearly derived from the noun and typically identifies what it is the noun does or what one does with the noun: *hand, father, water, fish*. Similarly some verbs are clearly derivative from adjectives (§4.2) and indicate the activity of making something like that description: *darken, simplify, enlarge, justify*.

Many verbs are irreducible lexical forms, i.e. their simple dictionary form cannot be analysed further into component parts: *think, walk, follow, create*, but not *justify, empower, characterise*. There are certain morphemes (prefixes and suffixes) which may help to form types of verbs. To *-ize* or *-ise* is often to make or cause something to be or become what the underlying root (§1.2.2) word means (usually a noun or adjective): *finalise, apologise, idolise*. Both the *en-* (*em-*) prefix and the *-en* suffix have a similar function: *enable, ensure, embitter, (en)lighten, strengthen*.

A small class of verb pairs have related forms (though separate lexemes) where one is a causative variation of the other: *rise : raise*; *fall : fell (a tree)*; *sit : seat*; *lie : lay*. This group is useful for demonstrating Hebrew causative conjugations. There are also pairs of unrelated lexemes where one is semantically a causative of the other: *eat : feed*; *die : kill*; *learn : teach*.

§3.3 Lexical and Auxiliary Verbs

There are two broad categories of verbs: an open-ended one of lexical verbs and a limited set of auxiliary verbs.

§3.3.1 Lexical Verbs

Lexical verbs are those that convey meaning. These account for most of the verbs in a dictionary — verbs like *show, give, sleep, crucify, disinherit*. All such verbs can be found in up to five inflectional forms in English: *show, shows, showing, showed, shown*. Some doubling up might restrict this to as few as three forms: *put, puts, putting*. These forms will be identified and explained below (§3.7.1).

§3.3.2 Auxiliary Verbs

Auxiliary verbs are those which are used along with lexical verbs in compound verbs (§3.4), or in truncated sentences (§3.4) apart from them, serving to locate a verb in terms of its voice, mood, tense and aspect (terms which will be explained below at §3.7.2-4). A few verbs can be used both as lexical verbs and as auxiliaries: *be, do, have, use*:

The land <u>has been given</u> to you.
You <u>do have</u> this going for you.
A prophet <u>used to be called</u> a seer.

There is also a limited set of modal auxiliary verbs: *can, could, will, would, shall, should, may, might, ought, must*. These are morphologically different from lexical verbs in that they lack some of the inflections seen in lexical verbs. Thus we cannot say **she is shalling, *they mighted*, or **he cans* (unless he happens to work in a canning factory!). Auxiliaries are also treated differently from lexical verbs in interrogation and negation (§6.1-2).

Hebrew and Greek make much less frequent use of auxiliary verbs, since many of the jobs that are done in English by auxiliaries are performed by the inflected verb forms.

§3.3.2.1 The Verb *Be*

The verb *be* and its functions deserve special consideration. This is the only verb in English with more than five distinct inflected forms. In addition to the simple form *be*, the gerund-participle form *being*, and the past-participle form *been*, we have *am* (first person singular present), *is* (third person singular present), *are* (second person singular and all plurals present), *was* (first and third person singular preterite), *were* (second person singular and all plurals preterite, and subjunctive form: §3.7.3.1.3).

The verb *be* can be used absolutely to predicate existence or presence:

The one who <u>is</u>, and who <u>was</u>, and who is to come.
Let it <u>be</u>, Lord.

More commonly in this sense it is preceded in English by a dummy word *there* (or followed by it in interrogative and some negative clauses), with consequent variation of the position of the subject:

<u>There are</u> still too many men.
<u>Is there</u> room in your father's house?
Nor <u>is there</u> an arbiter between us.

41

This use of *there* is to be distinguished from locative *there* (= *in that place*):

There are all the leaders of the north.

When used to express a relationship between a subject and another noun, adjective, or other phrase, the verb *be* is called the **copula** (link word):

The Son of Man is Lord of the Sabbath. (copula + predicative noun phrase complement)
When I am weak, then I am strong. (copula + adjective complement)
The Lamb will be in the city. (copula + prepositional phrase complement)

Some grammars speak of the verb *be* (and similarly *become*) taking a direct object as complement; we do sometimes find the accusative case after *be*:

That could be me! (Ezek 32:10 Message)

More traditional grammars say the verb *be* takes the same case after it as before it which means for a finite verb the nominative. Regardless of which case is used, we will call the complement of *be* a **predicative complement**:

You are a chosen people.
He is the Christ.
It is I. (formal or written English)

With a non-finite clause (e.g. where the predicator is an infinitive or participial form of *be* or *become*: §3.7.3.2.1.1, 3.7.3.2.2), the complement is in the accusative:

We don't want him to become our king.
He trained them to be princes.

The copula may have an adjective complement (the predicative use of the adjective: §4.2.7.2):

I was fearful.
Wisdom is better than rubies.

For these we could equally well use simple verbs in place of *be* + adjective complement:

I fear.
Wisdom excels rubies.

Greek and particularly Hebrew use a verb rather than copula + adjective more frequently than English in this situation. Such verbs may be called **stative** verbs as they express a state, or condition rather than an action, but the boundary between stative and active verbs is not hard and fast.

While the copula is generally expressed in English in independent clauses, some grammatical analyses regard the copula as being gapped in what are then construed as verbless embedded clauses:

God appointed him [to be] heir of all things.
I will make him [to be] faithful.
He wanted them [to be] put to death.
The king needs you [to be] here.

As an auxiliary verb, *be* is employed to create compound verbs (§3.4) to express a wider range of voices, moods and tense-aspects (§3.7) than is possible with just the handful of inflectional forms of lexical verbs available in English.

§3.3.2.2 The Verb *Do*

The verb *do* is both a lexical and an auxiliary verb. Compound verbs (§3.4) with *do* can be used to express more emphatic forms of verbal ideas (often because its opposite has been contemplated):

In fact, you <u>do love</u> all the brothers and sisters.
He insisted so strongly that they <u>did go</u> with him.

There is no equivalent compound verb form in Hebrew or Greek, which express emphasis in other ways.

The verb *do* can also function as a pro-form (a dummy verb) with no emphatic force to substitute for any lexical verb where the context allows:

'I didn't laugh.' 'Yes, you <u>did</u>.'

Do is also used (without any necessary emphatic force) in negation and interrogation (§6.1-2) as in the last example:

I <u>didn't</u> laugh.

§3.4 Compound Verbs

English frequently uses a combination of lexical and auxiliary verbs to fill the verb constituent slot of a clause, as in some of the examples above, in a cluster of up to four or occasionally more verb forms we will call a

compound verb. The elements of a compound verb can be interrupted by other constituents such as an adverb or (e.g. in interrogation: §6.2) the subject:

The money <u>could have been given</u> to the poor.

<u>May</u> it never <u>be</u> so!

What <u>must</u> I <u>do</u>?

If you do the right thing, <u>will</u> you not <u>be accepted</u>?

It is important then to be able to identify all of the elements of a compound verb even when the elements are not together. We can further analyse compound verbs into their component parts and give each part a technical label. However, at this stage it is better for our purposes to concentrate on the function of the whole compound verb in terms of the categories discussed below (voice, mood, tense and aspect), recognising that Hebrew and Greek may well use a single verb form (because their verbal systems are more highly inflected) where English must use a compound verb. Without the use of compound verbs, English has no future tense for example and no finite passive voice forms, but we will speak of such tense and voice existing in English because we will focus on the compound verb forms which make these possible. Thus while English verbs generally only have up to five inflected forms, the combinations with auxiliaries give us every bit as much flexibility and subtlety as Hebrew and Greek verbs achieve by different means. Compound verbs are sometimes labelled **periphrastic**, a term not particularly apt for English as it implies there is another way of saying the same thing with a single verb form (often not available in English). Hebrew and Greek do at times employ periphrastic constructions even when there is a roughly equivalent single inflected verb form.

Where the context allows, the lexical element may be gapped (omitted) from a compound verb, leaving just the auxiliary in a truncated expression:

Did you see him? If only I <u>had</u>!

Let come to me what <u>may</u>.

As it is in combinations with participles that compound verbs are often formed, we will defer further treatment of those parts of the verb conjugation that rely on participles (§3.7.3.2.2.2).

§3.5 Prepositional Verbs

A frequent type of verb in English is the **prepositional verb** or phrasal verb. A prepositional verb consists of a lexical verb + an obligatory prepositional form (or multiple prepositional forms) (§5.1):

He <u>handed over</u> the money.
They did not <u>give up</u> their evil ways.
I have <u>to look after</u> the sheep.

While it could appear that in the first example we have the verb <u>handed</u> + preposition *over* + prepositional complement *the money*, this is an unhelpful analysis. We could more helpfully say we have the verb *handed over* + direct object *the money*. So the verb + preposition combination has fused or grammaticalised into a single constituent. *Handed over* fills the slot that could otherwise be filled by a single lexical verb form such as *gave* or *transferred*. *Give up* could easily have been *abandon*. *Look after* might just as well have been *tend*. These single verb equivalents do not even need to exist in English in order to identify a prepositional verb. We can in some instances recognise a prepositional verb because we can place a direct object either after the whole verb phrase or between the elements of the verb phrase:

He <u>handed</u> the money <u>over</u>.

This fluidity of word order applies to some but not all prepositional verbs. A prepositional verb may undergo a passive transformation (§3.7.2.2). We can say:

The money was <u>handed over</u>.
The sheep have to be <u>looked after</u>.

We cannot, however, readily transform a verb + preposition which is not a prepositional verb:

Absalom stood beside the road.

cannot undergo a passive transformation to:

*The road was stood beside by Absalom.

Stand beside is not a prepositional verb. There will of course be grey areas and possible alternative analyses as a verb + preposition may be in process of grammaticalising into a prepositional verb:

They will <u>come after</u> them.

If *come after* means simply *follow*, it is probably verb + prepositional phrase; if it is intended in the sense of *pursue*, it may be felt as a prepositional verb.

It is going to be particularly helpful to think in terms of prepositional verbs, for the meaning of many Hebrew and Greek words will often be given as a number of alternatives, some of which are simple verbs, some of which are prepositional verbs. A Hebrew verb, for example, might be defined as *traverse*, *pass through*, or

45

a Greek verb as *hand over, betray* etc. Hebrew and more commonly Greek have some verbs which prefer to have a prepositional phrase as complement rather than a direct object. Greek has numerous verb forms compounded with one or more prepositional elements at the beginning.

§3.6 Transitive and Intransitive Verbs

Before discussing voice (§3.7.2) it will be helpful to consider the role of the verb as head of the predicate, or predicator. A verb (as other head words) may take an (optional) complement. Frequently this is in the form of a direct object, i.e. the person or thing most directly affected by the activity of the verb. Where a verb takes a direct object (§2.3.3.2.1) the verb is said to be **transitive**:

The Lord <u>loves</u> a cheerful giver.
So he <u>built</u> an altar.
Who <u>has done</u> this?

Some verbs can logically take two direct objects as their complement:

Joshua <u>made</u> them hewers of wood.
I <u>have appointed</u> him ruler.

Another way of viewing these is to think of the two objects as having an implied copula between them (§3.3.2.1) in which case the second object is predicative (§1.2.4.1).

I have appointed him (to be) ruler.

When preparing to learn another language, be aware that words which in English take a direct object may be expressed in the other language in some other form, such as an intransitive verb with indirect object or prepositional phrase. This is readily grasped if we realise that English has alternative ways of expressing similar concepts:

He addressed <u>them</u>. // He spoke <u>to them</u>.
They reached <u>the city</u>. // They came <u>to the city</u>.
She followed <u>him</u>. // She came <u>after him</u>.

An **intransitive** verb is one which does not have a direct object as complement.

The Spirit of God <u>moved</u> over the waters.
She <u>sat down</u>.

There can be no object to *moved* in this sense. Note that the same verb may often have a transitive as well as an intransitive sense:

Faith <u>moves</u> mountains. (transitive)
I <u>left</u> the cloak at Troas. (transitive)
He <u>left</u> and returned home. (intransitive)

§3.7 Verb Conjugation: Voice, Mood, Tense and Aspect

Verbs may be said to have the characteristics of voice, mood, tense and aspect. These categories are not alternatives to one another as though a verb can be either active (a voice) or indicative (a mood) or present (a tense). Each verb form may be described in terms of most or all of these categories. Thus the (compound) verb in:

His nephew <u>had been taken</u>.

is passive voice, indicative mood and pluperfect tense. Hebrew and Greek grammars conventionally set these out in a grid or **conjugation**. As you become familiar with the categories below you might try doing something similar for English verbs using a combination of the inflected forms and the auxiliaries, particularly forms of *will*, *be* and *have* for the more straightforward forms.

§3.7.1 The Inflected Verb Forms

English verbs are inflected to a limited extent, i.e. have several variations in form depending on their function in a sentence. Mostly these inflected forms follow reasonably predictable patterns, such as adding *-s* or *-ing* or *-(e)d* to the simple form, but a number of common English verbs have distinctive or irregular or 'strong' forms. We could call these forms the 'principal parts' of the English verb, though the term is more commonly applied to those Greek verb forms from which all other inflections may be derived. (See §3.3.2.1 for the additional forms of the verb *be*.)

§3.7.1.1 The Simple Form

The **simple form**, or bare form, e.g. *love, give, go* is the form you would find as the entry word (lemma) in a dictionary. The simple form is used for example for the infinitive (§3.7.3.2.1.1) or for where an active present tense verb (§3.7.3.1.5.1) has a first or second person subject or a plural subject.

§3.7.1.2 The Third Person Singular Form

The *-(e)s* form, e.g. *loves, gives, goes*, is restricted to the present tense of active indicative verbs where the subject is a **third person singular** (§3.7.3.1.1). In the case of the verb *have*, this reduces to *has*.

§3.7.1.3 The Gerund-Participle Form

The **gerund-participle** form, used for both gerunds (§3.7.3.2.1.2) and active present participles (§3.7.3.2.2), is formed by adding -*ing* to the simple verb (perhaps with some minor spelling modification), e.g. *loving, giving, going.*

§3.7.1.4 The Preterite Form

The **preterite** (used primarily as a past tense) is typically formed by adding -*(e)d* to the simple form (perhaps with some minor spelling modification). Some preterites ('strong' forms) undergo other changes, such as a stem change (*sing : sang*). Others exhibit no change (*hit : hit*). In the final example in the table below under 3.7.1.5, the unrelated preterite form *went* is 'borrowed' from another lexeme ('suppletion', a phenomenon that happens more frequently with Greek verbs).

§3.7.1.5 The Past-Participle Form

The **past-participle** forms exhibit a greater variety in their patterns. Many (and all new verbs formed) have their past-participle form identical with the preterite form with -*(e)d* but these functions are to be distinguished. Other past participles are formed with -*(e)n* or -*t*. Some are differentiated from simple forms and preterites by a vowel change or other variation. We may set out some preterites and past-participle forms thus:

Simple form	Preterite	Past-Participle
love	loved	loved
give	gave	given
spend	spent	spent
see	saw	seen
have	had	had
fly	flew	flown
think	thought	thought
eat	ate	eaten
sing	sang	sung
run	ran	run
put	put	put
go	went	gone

There are a few verbs with alternative past-participle forms, e.g. *got*, *gotten*; *struck*, *stricken*; *dragged*, *drug*. These variants are usually either dialectal or context-specific.

§3.7.2 Voice

Voice is the term used to indicate the relationship of the grammatical subject to the activity. English generally distinguishes two voices: active and passive.

Hebrew and Greek have active and passive verb forms analogous to English. They also have verb forms said to be in the middle voice, so this will be briefly introduced with English analogies.

§3.7.2.1 Active Voice

If the grammatical subject is the active performer, or the one experiencing the state or relationship, the verb is said to be **active**:

Cain <u>attacked</u> his brother.
You <u>have died</u> to sin.
<u>*Walk*</u> *in the way.*
He <u>rested</u> his head against a stone.
I <u>will give</u> you the keys of the kingdom.
I <u>became</u> impatient.
She <u>was</u> with me.

§3.7.2.2 Passive Voice

If the grammatical subject is on the receiving end of the activity (directly or occasionally indirectly), the verb is said to be in the **passive voice**. The past-participle form (§3.7.1.5) can by itself convey the passive voice in a non-finite clause:

Make everything according to the pattern <u>shown</u> you on the mountain.

For finite expressions in the passive, English needs to use the auxiliary *be*:

To each one of us grace <u>has been given</u>.
The bow <u>shall be seen</u> in the cloud.
You <u>are being built</u> into a spiritual house.

A passive verb is one which has undergone a passive transformation from a simpler canonical (§1.2.4.1.1) active expression. Only transitive verbs (§3.6) ordinarily undergo such a process, for what was the direct object of the active verb becomes the subject of the passive verb. What was the subject of the canonical active expression may or may not be expressed as an **agent** (personal) or **instrument** (impersonal) in the passive transformation:

They (subject) *were being baptised* (passive verb) *by John* (agent).

This is the passive transformation of:

John was baptising them.
You <u>have been washed</u>, you <u>have been sanctified</u>.
We <u>will be united</u> with him.
A person <u>is justified</u> by what he does and not by faith alone.
All things <u>were made</u> by him.

This is not to say that every time a passive is used, someone thought of the active form, then worked out how to transform it into a passive, but it is a helpful way of considering passives.

The passive voice (though sometimes frowned on in style guides) is a very useful vehicle for sentences where the focus is on the activity and the recipients of the activity rather than on the performer. In many instances, the performer is unknown, or simply not in focus. Where God is the implied performer of a passive verb in the Bible, such a verb is sometimes said to be a **divine passive** used for reverential reasons so as avoid the over-frequent use of God's name. This reasoning is doubtful and it is better to treat such passives along with others as simply placing the focus other than on the performer.

English also has the ability to make an **indirect passive** transformation, where it is the indirect object of the canonical active clause which becomes the subject of the passive verb. In this case the original direct object remains the object.

You <u>were shown</u> mercy. This transforms the active statement:
X (placeholder for the unstated performer) *showed you* (indirect object) *mercy* (direct object).
You <u>will be told</u> what to say.
I <u>have been given</u> a message for you.

§3.7.2.3 Middle Voice

English grammars do not usually speak of a **middle voice** (i.e. having some characteristics of both active and passive) but English can convey middle voice by compound verbs, or by the use of reflexive pronouns (§2.4.4), or by the use of simple verbs which inherently have a middle sense. Hebrew and Greek have some distinctive middle verb forms, some of which double up as passive forms so the term **medio-passive** is sometimes used. Middle verbs are those where some additional focus is given to the subject or where it is involved with the action of the verb as the implied direct or indirect object:

Join five curtains together (active).
Let me not join their assembly. (middle)
Their wings were joined to one another. (passive)

The middle example above effectively contemplates joining *myself* (referring back to the subject) to an assembly so there is a sense in which the subject is both performer and recipient of the action. There is some correlation between this middle sense and the intransitive sense of those verbs which can be used either transitively (with an object) or intransitively (§3.6):

Place me where I can feel the pillars. (transitive / active)
They felt sorry. (intransitive / formally active but with something of a 'middle' force as defined above)

§3.7.3 Mood

Mood in the grammatical sense of the word has little to do with how anyone is feeling on the day. **Mode** might have been a better descriptive label (the related adjective is **modal**). All lexical verbs can occur in a number of moods. Moods can be divided into finite and non-finite moods and all lexical verbs (but not auxiliaries) are found in both finite and non-finite forms.

§3.7.3.1 Finite Moods

Finite verbs are complete verbal expressions used for making statements (true, false, hypothetical), asking questions, expressing desire and issuing directives. They serve as the predicators in independent and finite embedded (dependent) clauses (§7.2). Grammatically, finite forms can be divided into **indicative** (declarative) and non-indicative or **irrealis** forms which will be dealt with in turn below. The verbs in the following sentences are all finite. Each sentence contains one verb which may be a compound (and some are split):

Love covers a multitude of sins.
He went up to the temple.
You will see me again.
Thus the heavens and the earth were completed.
They would outnumber the grains of sand.

When <u>will</u> the promise <u>be fulfilled</u>?
<u>Come</u>, *Lord Jesus.*
<u>May</u> *he never <u>leave</u> us.*

§3.7.3.1.1 Person, Number and Gender in Finite Moods

A feature of finite verbs is that they can be said to possess the characteristics (at least) of person (§2.4.1.1) and number (§2.3.1) in agreement with their subject. Generally in English this is simply a corollary of the person-number identity of the subject. Third person singular present active indicative verbs, however, do exhibit a distinctive inflected form in English (§3.7.1.2). Despite having one such marked person-number form, English must still generally express a subject:

Dominion belongs to the Lord and <u>he rules</u> over the nations.

No subject needs to be expressed with directives, however, which are understood to be second person:

Go and sin no more. or when the subject of a verb is gapped because it is implied from a previous clause:
Your law is perfect and <u>gives</u> understanding.

Even when no performer of the action is evident, English needs to employ the impersonal subject *it*:

<u>It</u> *was necessary.*
<u>It</u> *is not lawful to work on the Sabbath.*

All other active present person-number combinations use the simple form (other than for the verb *be*: §3.3.2.1).

I <u>am</u> the light of the world. (first person singular)
The heavens <u>declare</u> the glory of God. (third person plural)

Following is the full **paradigm** or **conjugation** grid of the active present indicative forms of a typical lexical verb *love* with the different person and number subjects.

singular	**first**	*I love*
	second	*you love*
	third	*he/she/it loves*
plural	**first**	*we love*
	second	*you love*
	third	*they love*

The only exception is with the singular use of *they* (§2.4.1.1), not commonly recognised in grammars, in which case the verb form used is the simple form (retained from its use with *they* as a plural).

Hebrew and Greek have distinct inflected forms for each of the person-number combinations of finite verbs, and do not need to express a pronoun subject independently (though they can do so). **Gender** (§2.3.2) does not enter into the discussion of English verbs. It makes no difference to the form of the verb whether the subject is male or female. Hebrew does make a morphological distinction in the verb according to gender for some verb forms.

§3.7.3.1.2 The Indicative Mood

The simplest mood is the **indicative**, used for making straightforward statements (positive or negative), or asking straightforward questions. It can also be used for hypothetical statements (though see §3.7.3.1.3).

I <u>desire</u> mercy not sacrifice.
Who <u>has known</u> the mind of the Lord?
I <u>will give</u> you this land.
Such a thing <u>has</u> never <u>been seen</u>.
If you <u>love</u> me, keep my commandments.

§3.7.3.1.3 Irrealis Forms and the Subjunctive Mood

❧ **Irrealis forms,** as their name suggests, are those where the speaker does not affirm the reality of an event. It may be conditional, or hypothetical, or desired, rather than a simple statement of fact or a question eliciting an answer based on reality. One irrealis form is the **subjunctive mood**, though its use is declining. The subjunctive mood takes two forms: the simple form of the verb (with no -*s* inflection for third person singular) and the preterite form (but note *were* is used for all person–number forms of the verb be). While these forms are used mostly in some embedded (subordinate) clauses, particularly conditional (§7.2.3.8), concessive (§7.2.3.9) and indirect questions (§7.2.1.2), they are occasionally found in independent clauses:

Long <u>live</u> the king!
Far <u>be</u> it from me!
If only it <u>were</u> evening!
<u>Were</u> I to tell of them, they would be more than can be counted.
When he hides his face, who can behold him, whether it <u>be</u> a nation or an individual?

(action) act or state of being in act
a fact

Though he <u>slay</u> me, yet will I trust in him. (Job 13:15 KJV)
We grope as if we <u>had</u> no eyes.

A greater range of irrealis mood forms can be realised with compound verbs which include the modal auxiliaries *would, should, can, could, may, might*:

Oh, that I <u>might have</u> my request.
<u>Would that</u> all the Lord's people <u>were</u> prophets.
<u>May</u> the king <u>live</u> forever.
He promised to give her whatever she <u>should ask</u>.

> Hebrew and Greek have irrealis verb forms often rendered by English subjunctives or with the aid of modal auxliaries. Hebrew has jussive and cohortative forms and Greek has a subjunctive and a rarer optative mood.

§3.7.3.1.4 The Imperative Mood and Directives

The mood used for expressing **directives** (direct commands, pleas, prayers) is the **imperative mood**. English uses the simple form (§3.7.1.1) for active imperatives:

<u>Think</u> on these things.
<u>Be</u> a man.
<u>Do</u> this, and you will live.
<u>Grant</u> me this one request.

Directives can be issued in the passive with imperative *be* + past participle:

<u>Be warned</u>.
First <u>be reconciled</u> to your brother.

The subject of a direct command is second person (whether expressed as a pronoun or, more generally, left unexpressed). There may be a noun in the vocative (§2.3.3.2.5) in apposition (§2.3.3.1) with the implied subject, though the vocative word is not the subject:

<u>Lord</u>, hear our prayer.

Directives or obligations placed on a third party are also possible and can be realised in a variety of ways in English:

<u>Let</u> him <u>continue</u> to be evil.
She <u>is to remain</u> unmarried.
They <u>must purify</u> themselves.

Hebrew and Greek both have imperative forms closely corresponding in function to the English imperative. Greek has a third person imperative form used for directives aimed at third parties best rendered by such expressions as *Let him depart; she is to come.*

§3.7.3.1.5 Tense in Finite Verb Forms

Grammars vary as to whether they use the word **tense** to refer to a form (e.g. the preterite form: §3.7.1.4) or to the time reference of the verb (for the correlation is far from cosy) or for a combination of the functions of time and aspect (§3.7.4). There are three basic tenses or times that can be envisaged: present, past and future, i.e. generally from the speaker's or writer's perspective. A rare exception is the occasional use of **epistolary** tenses where the writer projects himself or herself into the reader's timeframe: *I sent him therefore the more carefully.* (Phil 2:28 KJV; the emissary had not been sent at the time of writing.)

§3.7.3.1.5.1 Present Time

For the active present tense, English uses the simple form of the verb (§3.7.1.1) for all but third person singular, which has the inflectional -(e)s form (§3.7.1.2):

You lack nothing.
This bread gives life.

Besides denoting an action or state that is current, the present tense can denote a recurrent event. The use of the present tense form for statements which hold true at all times is called the **gnomic present**:

The sun rises in the east.
The righteous give generously.

§3.7.3.1.5.2 Past Time

The simplest way of indicating events in the past is by the use of the preterite form of the verb (§3.7.1.4).

I saw the Lord.
Abraham believed God.

English also occasionally uses its present tense forms for events in the past, which we may call the **historic present**. In English this is particularly used where the past action is regarded as having a continuous effect:

I hear that there are divisions among you.
For Moses writes about the righteousness that is by the law ...

The latter use is also sometimes called the **literary present**.

§3.7.3.1.5.3 Future Time

The expression of future events in English is generally effected by the use of the modal auxiliaries *will* and *shall* or with other compound expressions such as *be about to, be going to, intend to*:

I *will come* to you soon.
I *intend to build* a house for the name of the Lord my God.
Shall I *hide* from Abraham what I *am about to do*?

Futures may also be expressed by the simple (present) form and particularly by the imperfective (continuous) form with *be* + the gerund-participle form:

Tomorrow *is* the new moon.
His mother said to the servants, 'Do whatever he *tells* you.'
I will make all the kingdoms of the earth horrified at what *happens* to you.
Yes, I *am coming* soon!

§3.7.3.1.5.4 Perfect and Related Tense Forms

There is also (using compound verb forms with *have*) a set of **perfect** (or perfective-stative or resultative) verb forms: the **present perfect** (or simply the perfect) tense, the **pluperfect** (or past perfect) tense, and the **future perfect** tense. These focus on the resulting experience of the actor, or consequence of an action, and the time reference in the tense designations relates to the time of the consequence rather than the action itself:

Christ *has conquered* death. (present perfect; i.e. a present consequence of a past action is in view)
The Lord *had opened* a door for me. (pluperfect; i.e. a past consequence of a prior action is in view).
He will die for his sin; but you *will have saved* yourself. (future perfect; i.e. a future consequence of a prior action is in view.)

Greek has a distinctive set of perfect and related tense forms closely corresponding in function to English perfects. The tense often called 'perfect' in Hebrew has a wider function, including the resultative or consequential meaning of the English perfect.

§3.7.3.2 Non-finite Moods

English has several non-finite verb forms. These may not constitute the predicators of independent clauses, but may serve as predicators of non-finite dependant clauses. The non-finite verb forms in English are the infinitive, the gerund and the participle.

§3.7.3.2.1 Verbal Nouns

As well as nouns formed from verbal roots (§2.2), there are in English two inflectional forms of **verbal nouns** capable of being formed from any lexical verb: the infinitive and the gerund. Verbal nouns, as their name suggests, display characteristics of both verbs and nouns.

§3.7.3.2.1.1 The Infinitive

An **infinitive** is a non-finite verb form; that is it cannot alone be the predicator of a finite or independent clause. English infinitives are of two types, **bare infinitives** (using the simple form of the verb, such as *show, give, crucify*) and *to-***infinitives** where the simple form of the verb is preceded by *to*. We will consider the *to* to be part of the verb.

Hebrew often uses an equivalent to English *to* with infinitives; Greek does not.

The form of the verb used after modal auxiliaries is generally the bare infinitive form (§3.7.3.2.1.1):

Teach me the way I should go.
No-one can tame the tongue.
You must be born again.

However, after *ought, use, need, be* and *have* (the latter two only in the sense of obligation), the *to*-infinitive form is used:

You ought to endure suffering.
Moses used to put a veil over his face.
He had to pass through Samaria.
This month is to be for you the first month.

As verbal nouns, infinitives can occupy the slot otherwise occupied by nouns in the clause structure such as the subject slot:

To obey is better than sacrifice.
To show partiality is not good.

Infinitives can be considered to form the complement, including direct object, of many verbs (*decide, want, forbid, encourage, continue, choose, seem* etc.), even when another object is present:

He will do everything I want him <u>to do</u>.
Even what they seem <u>to have</u> will be taken away.
I watched Satan <u>fall</u> from heaven. (bare infinitive)
I desire <u>to argue</u> my case with God.

The fact that *to argue*, for example, can be regarded as the object of *desire* is demonstrable by comparing the following sentence (with simple noun object):

I desire <u>an argument</u> with God.

A frequent use of *to*-infinitive clauses in English is to express purpose (cf. §7.2.3.6):

He did this <u>to show</u> his righteousness.
I have written to you <u>to encourage</u> you.

A *to*-infinitive may form the complement of some nouns (generally those with some verbal force):

There was no need <u>to stab</u> him again.
We have encouragement <u>to hold fast</u> to this hope.

A *to*-infinitive may also form the complement of some adjectives:

And you were worthy <u>to learn</u> this secret.
I think it right <u>to refresh</u> your memory.

These bare and *to*-infinitives are active in voice (§3.7.2.1). English lacks a single verb form for infinitives other than the active form. Other voice-tense-aspect infinitives may be formed with auxiliaries:

They claim <u>to be prophesying</u> in my name. (active imperfective)
It is better <u>to be persecuted</u> for doing good than for doing evil. (passive perfective)
A Lamb that appeared <u>to have been killed</u>. (passive perfect)

We may speak of an infinitive as being the predicator of a non-finite clause. The subject of such an infinitive, if expressed, may be an accusative word in the matrix clause (§7.2):

Let's get <u>him to drink</u> wine again tonight.
I know <u>you to be</u> expert in all the customs and disputes of the Jews.

As with other verb forms, an infinitive can in turn take a complement such as a direct or indirect object:

Allow us <u>to make a treaty</u> with you. (infinitive + direct object)
The land he swore to your fathers <u>to give you</u>. (infinitive + indirect object)
Go to my relatives <u>to find my son</u> (infinitive + indirect object) *<u>a wife</u>* (direct object).

Infinitives, like other verb forms, may be modified by adverbs:

Be careful <u>never to take</u> my son back there.
It is better to be satisfied than <u>always to crave</u> more.

In a truncated idiom, the infinitival form may be reduced to *to*:

Though you used <u>to</u>, you no longer worship idols.
I wished to come but was unable <u>to</u>.

§3.7.3.2.1.2 The Gerund

The other verbal noun form in English is the **gerund**. This use of the gerund-participle form (*-ing*) is to be distinguished from its use as a participle (§3.7.3.2.2). A gerund is a noun with verbal characteristics. It is often capable of being paraphrased by *the act of -ing*. Gerund-participle forms that follow prepositions such as *to, of, with, without, by, by means of, through* are likely to be gerunds:

With the <u>coming</u> of dawn ...
The gift of God's grace was given me by the <u>working</u> of his power.

As a noun, a gerund may occupy any constituent slot of subject or oblique cases:

His <u>anointing</u> teaches you about all things. (subject)
I have heard the <u>groaning</u> of the Israelites. (direct object)
Nothing can prevent the Lord from <u>delivering</u>. (prepositional complement)

Note from the above examples a gerund (unlike an English infinitive) may be determined e.g. by an article or a possessive form.

A gerund may also be modified by an adjective:

Deacons must be dignified, not two-faced, not given to <u>excessive drinking</u>.

or by an adverb:

He raised her up by <u>gently taking</u> her hand.
It is unreasonable to send a prisoner without <u>clearly indicating</u> the charges against him.

As with infinitives, the subject of the gerund (if expressed, which it is more rarely than with infinitives) is in the accusative case:

Death prevented <u>them continuing</u> in office.
They stopped <u>him prophesying</u>.

In the above two examples, possessive forms *their* and *his* could be substituted (in a somewhat more formal register) for the accusatives *them* and *him*. Compare:

With him we are sending the brother who is famous among all the churches for his <u>proclaiming</u> the good news. (2 Cor 8:18 NRSV)

As a non-finite verbal form, a gerund may take a complement, i.e. be the predicator of a non-finite (dependent) clause:

God has rejected you from <u>being king</u> over Israel. (gerund + predicative complement)
I have killed a man for <u>wounding me</u>. (gerund + direct object)
The Lord has blessed his people by <u>giving them</u> (gerund + indirect object) *<u>food</u>* (direct object).
That is why I have kept you from <u>sinning against me</u>. (gerund + prepositional phrase)

> What Hebrew and Greek may lack in a distinctive gerund form, they make up for with a greater use of the infinitive form of the verbal noun to do many of the things that a gerund does in English. They may, for example, unlike English infinitives but like English gerunds, be preceded by prepositions and determinatives. You may then translate them using English gerunds, or other nouns with verbal roots, or turn the clause into a finite clause. The following roughly equivalent sentences illustrate the point:
>
> *<u>To obey</u> is better than sacrifice.* (infinitive)
> *<u>Obeying</u> is better than sacrifice.* (gerund)
> *<u>Obedience</u> is better than sacrifice.* (noun with verbal root)
> *Better than sacrifice is <u>that we are obedient</u>.* (finite clause)

§3.7.3.2.2 The Participle

A **participle** is a non-finite verb form and may be said to constitute the predicator of a non-finite clause, as well as functioning in combination with auxiliaries to form compound finite verbs. Some grammars describe participles as verbal adjectives, though their adjectival role is only one aspect of their function. As noted above (§3.7.1.3, §3.7.1.5), English has two participial forms, the gerund-participle (invariably ending in -*ing*), and the past-participle, with more varied forms and functions. As predicator of a non-finite clause, a participle may be said to have a subject, i.e. a noun (subject or oblique case word) of the matrix clause (§7.2) functions as the head of the participial clause:

The women went to the tomb, <u>taking</u> the spices. (subject of present participle is subject of matrix clause [§7.2]: *women*)

A man found him <u>wandering</u> in the field. (subject of participle is direct object of matrix clause (§7.2: *him*)

If you see a donkey <u>fallen</u> on the road. (subject of participle is direct object of matrix clause: *donkey*)

Grant those <u>suffering</u> relief from their distress. (subject of participle is indirect object of matrix clause [§7.2: *those*])

He sought alms from those <u>going</u> into the temple. (subject of participle is prepositional complement of matrix clause [§7.2: *those*])

> Hebrew and Greek make use of participles in many of the same ways as English. Participles are a particularly frequent phenomenon of Greek style where they are often used for backgrounded information.

§3.7.3.2.2.1 Voice and Tense in Participles

The gerund-participle form (-*ing*) is used as an active present participle and typically expresses an action taking place at the same time as the verb in the matrix clause (§7.2; i.e. not necessarily in present time from the speaker's perspective):

<u>Looking up</u> to heaven, he gave thanks. (participle is contemporary with past action)

You will meet a man <u>carrying</u> three young goats. (participle is contemporary with future action)

The present participle may also be used for an action which more or less immediately precedes the action of the main verb:

And <u>hearing</u> the multitude pass by, he asked what it meant. (Luke 18:36 KJV)

cf.:

When he heard the crowd going by, he asked what was happening. (Luke 18:36 NIV2011)

Likewise the present participle may in some contexts express imminent future action:

His thunder announces the <u>coming</u> storm.

A past participle used independently of auxiliaries is generally passive in voice and indicates the resultant state of the person or thing acted upon:

See that you make them according to the pattern <u>shown</u> you on the mountain.
They have dug their own cisterns, <u>broken</u> cisterns that cannot hold water.

A few past participles are active in meaning, e.g. *grown, fallen, dead, gone*. Despite its name, the past-participle has no inherent tense (i.e. for the state, though of course the action which produced it is prior).

As predicator of its non-finite clause, a participle may have a complement including a direct or indirect object or prepositional phrase:

<u>*Taking her hand*</u>*, he said, 'Arise'.* (present participle + direct object)
He loves the foreigner, <u>giving him food and clothing</u>. (present participle + indirect object + direct object)
They carried out their responsibilities according to the regulations <u>given them by their ancestor Aaron</u>. (past participle + indirect object + prepositional phrase)
They saw Jesus <u>walking on the water</u>. (present participle + prepositional phrase)
I give my opinion as one <u>shown mercy by the Lord</u>. (past participle + direct object + prepositional phrase)

§3.7.3.2.2.2 Compound Verbs with Participles

The following sets out the main types of compound verbs with participles to express a finite verb.

Forms of the verb *be* + present participle constitute active imperfective tense-aspect constructions (§3.7.4):

We <u>are waiting for</u> new heavens and a new earth. (active present imperfective)
You <u>were running</u> a good race. (active past imperfective)
He <u>will be winnowing</u> barley. (active future imperfective)

Forms of the verb *be* + past participle constitute passive tense-aspect constructions (§3.7.4):

We <u>are found</u> to be false witnesses. (passive present perfective)
This one <u>will be called</u> woman, for out of man this one <u>was taken</u>. (passive future perfective … passive past perfective)

Forms of the verb *have* + past participle constitute active perfect tense-aspect constructions (§3.7.4):

We <u>have taken</u> a vow. (active present perfect)
The Lord <u>had spoken</u> to Moses. (active pluperfect)
He will die for his sin, but you <u>will have saved</u> yourself. (active future perfect)

Forms of the verbs *have* + *be* + past participle constitute passive perfect tense-aspect constructions (§3.7.4):

But to each one of us grace <u>has been given</u>. (passive present perfect)
The whole nation <u>had been circumcised</u>. (passive pluperfect)
In the days to come all <u>will have been</u> long <u>forgotten</u>. (passive future perfect)

§3.7.3.2.2.3 Participle as Adjective and Noun

The participle may assume an adjectival quality, being used to modify nouns particularly in the attributive position (§4.2.7.1):

Give this to the <u>commanding</u> officer.
This is a <u>binding</u> ordinance.
They picked up the <u>broken</u> pieces.

If used in the predicative position (§4.2.7.2), such participles are often indistinguishable from the compound verb form discussed above (§3.7.3.2.2).

This ordinance <u>is binding</u>. = This ordinance binds.
The wall of Jerusalem <u>is broken down</u>. = The wall of Jerusalem has been broken down.

A participle may be used **substantivally** (i.e. as a noun) to refer to the person or thing performing that action or undergoing that state. This is not to be confused with the gerund (identical in form: §3.7.3.2.1.2) which refers to the action performed or the state undergone:

Let the <u>discerning</u> get guidance. (present participle as noun).
Write the <u>following</u>. (present participle as noun).
I will bandage the <u>injured</u> (past participle as noun).
They will face a reckoning (gerund) *before Jesus Christ who stands ready to*

judge the <u>living</u> (present participle as noun) *and the <u>dead</u>* (past participle as noun).

Participles, like other verb forms, may be modified by adverbs:

A land that drinks in the rain <u>often falling</u> on it.
You should open your hand, <u>willingly lending</u> enough to meet the need.
There was a <u>freshly plucked</u> olive leaf in its beak.
Like apples of gold in settings of silver is a word <u>skilfully spoken</u>.

§3.7.3.2.2.4 Absolute Use of the Participle

It is possible to have as the head or subject of the participial clause a noun which is not a constituent of the matrix clause (§7.2; i.e. the participle and its subject are hanging, or **absolute**:

<u>God willing</u>, I will come to you soon.
See the devastation of that land, <u>nothing planted</u>, <u>nothing sprouting</u>.

> Greek has a similar idiom, the genitive absolute, in which the noun and participle are in the genitive case.

§3.7.3.2.2.5 Translating Participles

Where participles are used in Hebrew or particularly Greek where they are abundant, English style often prefers to render them by a full clause. Consider the following translations of Acts 21:2:

And finding a ship sailing over unto Phenicia, we went aboard, and set forth. (participle; KJV)
We found a ship crossing over to Phoenicia, went on board and set sail. (co-ordinate clause; NIV2011)
When we found a ship bound for Phoenicia, we went on board and set sail. (subordinate clause; NRSV)

§3.7.4 Verbal Aspect

Older grammars defined **verbal aspect** in terms of the type of action described (punctiliar, repeated, etc.). This is now more accurately described as Aktionsart. Aspect now indicates the stance of the speaker with regard to the action. The same writer might relate an event using a perfective aspect at one point and an imperfective aspect at another, not because the action itself is any different but because the stance of the speaker with regard to the action is different. Is the action viewed as a whole, even though the event itself may be ongoing or recurrent, or is it viewed as a staged process?

The situation with aspect is rather complicated for two reasons. First there are different theories on how significant a role aspect plays, whether in English or in the biblical languages. The approach adopted here is that in all these languages there is a subtle interplay of tense (§3.7.3.1.5) and aspect; hence we may speak of the feature of tense-aspect. In each language the situation has been evolving over time, so the same form may be used with more tense (time) indication or more aspect indication in different periods. There is no simple direct correlation between form (whether inflectional or a compound verb form) and tense-aspectual force. A verb form like *attend* (see examples below) could be perfective in one context and imperfective in another.

The second complicating factor is that there are different descriptive systems for covering aspect. The following will adopt a twofold aspectual categorisation of perfective and imperfective.

We could regard the default or unmarked aspect as **perfective** (not to be confused with the perfect tense system: §3.7.3.1.5.4), or **aoristic** (a Greek word meaning undefined). This looks at an action as a whole 'from the outside':

Attend to my cry, O Lord.
I find this man not guilty.
In the beginning God created the heavens and the earth.

Imperfective verbs express the speaker's contemplation of an action more as a process ('from within') taking place in present, past or future time. Adverbs like *continually* or *regularly* may aid the perception of imperfective aspect:

Happy are these your servants, who continually attend you.
Every day of his life he dined regularly in the king's presence.

In English, the imperfective or continuous aspect of the verb may be rendered more explicitly by the use of compound verbs with forms of *be* or *keep* + present participle, or, with somewhat different nuances, *try* or *use* + *to*-infinitive or *begin* + present participle or *to*-infinitive:

I am not running in vain.
They were sleeping.
Two women will be grinding with a mill.
They used to come up to Jerusalem each year.
She stood up and began praising God.

The perfect set of verb tenses (§3.7.3.1.5.4) may also be in imperfective aspect:

The whole creation <u>has been groaning</u> in labour pains until now. (present perfect imperfective; the present consequence of an action viewed from within as a process)

By then, he <u>had been fasting</u> for forty days. (pluperfect imperfective; i.e. past consequence of an action viewed from within as a process)

The role of aspect is a very live discussion in contemporary grammars of Hebrew and Greek. Hebrew has two fundamental tense-aspect forms, often labelled the perfect and the imperfect, which must do service for a wide range of tense-aspect combinations. Greek has some distinctive perfective (aoristic) and imperfective aspectual forms.

Exercises for Chapter 3

1. Identify the finite verbs in the following; show all the elements of a compound verb:

   a. *Jesus healed many who had various diseases.*

   b. *A voice of one calling in the wilderness, 'Prepare the way of the Lord.'*

   c. *Who am I that I should go to Pharaoh and bring the Israelites out of Egypt?*

   d. *Paul, a servant of Christ Jesus, called to be an apostle and set apart for the gospel of God.*

   e. *All have sinned and fall short of the glory of God.*

   f. *Even if I thought there was still hope for me, even if I had a husband tonight and then gave birth to sons, would you wait until they grew up?*

   g. *Gather around so I can tell you what will happen to you in days to come.*

2. Which of the following underlined verbs are intransitive (in this sense)?

   a. *You <u>are</u> able <u>to give</u> interpretations and <u>solve</u> difficult problems.*

   b. *Anyone who <u>runs</u> ahead and does not <u>continue</u> in the teaching of Christ does not <u>have</u> God.*

   c. *You <u>were running</u> a good race.*

   d. *He <u>sat down</u> at the right hand of the throne of God.*

   e. *When he <u>opened</u> his eyes he <u>could see</u> nothing.*

   f. *While he <u>was sleeping</u>, he <u>took</u> one of the man's ribs and then <u>closed up</u> the place with flesh.*

   g. *Jesus I <u>know</u>, and Paul I know, but who <u>are</u> you?*

h. *I <u>was given</u> a thorn in my flesh.*

3. Turn the following passive clauses into their canonical active (and positive) form. If the agent is unstated, mark the subject with X:

a. *He was vindicated by the Spirit.*

b. *The floodgates of the heavens were opened.*

c. *You will never be released from service as woodcutters and water carriers.*

d. *You also, like living stones, are being built into a spiritual house.*

4. Identify and distinguish between the participles and gerunds in the following (including those participles that are part of a compound verb):

a. *To answer before listening, that is folly and shame.*

b. *A man found him wandering around in the fields and asked him, 'What are you looking for?'*

c. *For we are God's handiwork, created in Christ Jesus to do good works, which God prepared in advance for us to do.*

d. *He said this in the hearing of the people.*

e. *Finding a fresh jawbone of a donkey, he grabbed it and struck down a thousand men.*

f. *If you knew the gift of God and who it is that asks you for a drink, you would have asked him and he would have given you living water.*

g. *Solomon showed his love for the Lord by walking according to the instructions given him by his father David.*

h. *For as lightning that comes from the east is visible in the west, so will be the coming of the Son of Man.*

5. Parse the underlined verb forms (give a description of them in terms of voice, mood, tense, aspect, person and number where relevant); analyse compound verbs (unbroken underline) as a whole:

a. *I <u>will make</u> him <u>want</u> <u>to return</u> to his own country.*

b. *<u>Lift up</u> your heads, you gates; <u>be lifted up</u>, you ancient doors.*

c. *But you <u>were washed</u>, you <u>were sanctified</u>, you <u>were justified</u>.*

d. *His head and hands <u>had been broken off</u> and <u>were lying</u> on the threshold.*

e. *You <u>are</u> responsible for the wrong I <u>am suffering</u>.*

f. *Christ <u>was sacrificed</u> once <u>to take away</u> the sins of many.*

g. *Pilate <u>ordered</u> that it <u>be given</u> to him.*

4. Determinatives, Adjectives and Adverbs: Some More Descriptive Words

Several classes of words serve as determiners or modifiers of other constituents. They serve to identify, nuance, or define more precisely the other elements.

§4.1 Determinatives

Determinatives belong to a more recently recognised category of parts of speech. They have sometimes been loosely thought of as a subcategory of adjectives (§4.2), since, like adjectives, they serve as adjuncts to noun phrases, though their role is more to do with identification and delimitation than description. In their determinative function they are incapable of being used in the predicative (§4.2.7.2) position: s*ome people,* but not **People were some.*

Languages may employ a variety of strategies to introduce identification to noun phrases and in particular to mark them as to their degree of definiteness. The principal dedicated determinatives in English are the **definite article** *the* and the **indefinite article** *a* (*an*). Other words that might be used as determinatives (though most have other functions as well) are *some, any, all, several, enough, sufficient, each, every, either, neither, other, another, a few, a little, a certain, this, that, these, those, which, what, much, many, most, no* together with the possessive forms *my, your, David's* etc. and the numerals, *one, two* etc.

§4.1.1 The Use of Determinatives

Unlike some languages, English does not require a determinative before all nouns. Plurals of any noun class may readily be expressed without a determinative, though they may take a determinative, of which the default is *some*:

At that time <u>people</u> began to invoke the name of the Lord.
<u>Some</u> shepherds came and drove them away.

Uncountable nouns, such as abstract nouns (§2.1.1), may readily be used in the singular without a determinative:

May <u>mercy</u>, <u>peace</u>, and <u>love</u> be yours in <u>abundance</u>.
Show me <u>kindness</u> and <u>faithfulness</u>.

though determinatives (such as possessive forms) may be used with abstract nouns:

Do not ever cut off <u>your</u> kindness from my family.
<u>His</u> faithfulness endures to all generations.

Countable nouns generally require a determinative in the singular:

He put them on <u>a</u> donkey.
Stay here with <u>the</u> donkey.

When articles and other determinatives are used, they always come before the noun they determine, whether immediately, or with a modifier (such as an adjective or adjectival phrase) intervening:

<u>Its</u> brilliance was like that of <u>a</u> very precious jewel.
Then <u>the</u> angel blew <u>his</u> trumpet.
<u>This</u> teaching is hard!
<u>Those</u> brothers who are with me greet you.
<u>Some</u> Hebrews crossed <u>the</u> fords of <u>the</u> Jordan.
By this <u>all</u> people will know that you are <u>my</u> disciples.

Coordinated words (§5.2) which share a determinative are generally felt to belong more closely together:

<u>The</u> poor and needy,

but:

<u>the</u> poor and <u>the</u> oppressor.
<u>His</u> flocks and herds,

but:

<u>our</u> children and <u>our</u> cattle.

§4.1.2 Concord in Determinatives

Determinatives may demonstrate **concord** or grammatical agreement with the noun they determine in such qualities as number, gender and case. In English only number is so marked and only in a few instances. The deictic (pointing out) determinatives *this* and *that* are singular and have corresponding plurals *these* and *those*:

Heal the sick in <u>that</u> town.
You know <u>these</u> people.
He will discover in <u>those</u> records that <u>this</u> city is rebellious.

The determinative *both* is inherently dual (§2.3.1) in that it only determines a noun representing two of something:

<u>Both</u> *dreams of Pharaoh have the same meaning.*

See below (§4.1.4) for the indefinite article *a* (*an*) which is only used with singular nouns.

> Hebrew and Greek, being more highly inflected languages, may be expected to show more concord between at least some determinatives and their nouns in such qualities as gender and (for Greek) case, in addition to number.

§4.1.3 The Definite Article

By far the most frequently occurring determinative (in English and the biblical languages) is the **definite article** *the*. Note that though the use of the definite article can assist in identifying a noun phrase as definite (having a specific referent), it is not the essential ingredient of a definite noun phrase. Proper nouns are inherently definite and the possessive forms <u>David's</u> *son*, <u>his</u> *friend* (as distinct from *a son of David, a friend of his*) identify definite noun phrases.

Key uses of the definite article are:

1) the unique referent use, i.e. when there is only one referent to be considered:

He causes <u>the</u> sun to rise on the evil and the good.

2) the use of the definite article before some titles, some artistic creations such as literary works, some unique or regularly recurrent events, festivals and movements:

<u>The</u> *Book of the Wars of <u>the</u> Lord.*
<u>The</u> *Feast of Unleavened Bread.*
<u>The</u> *emperor.*

3) the deictic use, i.e. when in the context the referent is identifiable because it is on view or known to be at hand:

David said to the priest Abiathar, 'Bring me <u>the</u> ephod.'

4) the anaphoric use, i.e. to introduce a noun that has already been introduced (or is about to be further identified):

They saddled a donkey for him and he mounted <u>the</u> donkey.
If you see <u>the</u> donkey of someone who hates you …

Proper nouns (§2.1.2), when names of persons or places do not normally take a definite article in English other than in this type of construction:

This is <u>the</u> Moses who said to the Israelites …

5) the generic use, i.e. to refer to a typical member of a class:

You shall not eat these: <u>the</u> camel, <u>the</u> hare, and <u>the</u> rock badger.

> A word preceded by the article is said to be **articular**. A word without the article is said to be **anarthrous**. Whether a noun is articular or anarthrous can have a bearing on interpretation, particularly in Greek.
>
> English avoids the use of both an article and some other determinatives, such as possessives and deictics: **the my house, *the this book*. Hebrew and Greek are both happy to use the article in combination with such other determinatives.

§4.1.3.1 The Definite Article before Adjectives and Adverbs

The definite article *the* (or *all the*) may also be used with a comparative adjective (§4.2.6.2) and with a comparative or superlative adverb (§4.3.3):

I am <u>all the more eager</u> to send him to you.
<u>The more</u> the words, <u>the less</u> the meaning.
Therefore I will boast <u>all the more gladly</u> about my weaknesses.
<u>The longer</u> we wait, <u>the more joyful</u> our hope.
I am not <u>the least</u> ashamed.

This usage is not to be confused with the substantival use of the comparative or superlative adjective which may also involve the use of the definite article (§4.2.8).

§4.1.4 The Indefinite Article

The **indefinite article** *a* (or *an* before vowel sounds: §1.2.1) is a fossilised form of the numeral *one*. It is used generally with countable nouns in the singular:

We have <u>a</u> father, <u>an</u> old man.

Where an indefinite article is used with an abstract noun (§2.1.1), it is likely to be in the sense of *an instance of …* or *a type of …*:

For he never thought of doing <u>a kindness</u>.
… not having <u>a righteousness</u> of my own that comes from the law.

Hebrew and Greek both have a close equivalent of the definite article but lack a real equivalent of the indefinite article (though we do find an indefinite expression which may be translated *a certain*). Thus if we have a Hebrew or Greek word for *woman* or *edict* (without an article or other determinative) it might be better translated *a woman* or *an edict*.

§4.1.5 Other Determinatives

Other examples of determinative use follow. Note that they are only determinatives when they serve to identify a noun phrase. Other uses of the same words might be considered as pronouns or adjectives and older English grammars (and textbooks of Hebrew and Greek) which do not recognise the category of determinatives will of necessity treat even the instances below under some other category:

No shrub of the field had yet appeared.
I will pour out my Spirit on all people.
You will be the father of many nations.
Two men, one on either side.
Which way did he go?
Men of Israel, and you Gentiles who fear God, listen.

Hebrew and Greek have analogous determinatives, though the term may not be used in the grammars. Some are treated as pronouns and some as adjectives.

§4.2 Adjectives

Adjectives serve to further modify or nuance nouns. Whereas we may have several different nouns to represent what is broadly categorised as a *rock* (*stone*, *pebble*, *boulder*, *gem* etc.), we lack nouns to describe all the more subtle differences in size, shape, colour, condition etc. Adjectives supply this lack and give tremendous descriptive power to language.

A typical adjective is the adjective of quality which describes a physical or evident characteristic (such as size, colour, age, material, condition, demeanour):

Like a gold ring in a pig's snout is a beautiful woman who abandons discretion.
The nations worship their gods on the high mountains and hills and under every green tree.
The jar of flour was never empty.
You hunt me as a fierce lion.

To this we may add other less tangible categories such as origin, duration, or intellectual, moral and spiritual qualities:

Every inclination of the thoughts of their minds was <u>evil</u> all the time.
Brothers and sisters, partners in a <u>heavenly</u> calling.
You will live a <u>long</u> time in the land.
I listened closely to your <u>wise</u> thoughts.
The Lord abhors <u>dishonest</u> scales.

§4.2.1 Adjectives or Determinatives

Some other words often treated in grammars as adjectives include number words (<u>forty</u> *days, the* <u>second</u> *month*), possessive forms (<u>my</u> *husband,* <u>your</u> *transgressions,* <u>their own</u> *straw*), deictics or demonstratives (<u>that</u> *land,* <u>these</u> *women*), interrogatives (<u>which</u> *way? by* <u>what</u> *name?*) and exclamatives (<u>what</u> *misfortune!*). These are treated above under the category of determinatives (§4.1).

§4.2.2 Adjective Formation

Adjectives may be irreducible lexical words in their own right or may be formed from other words in a number of ways. Adjectives may simply be identical with related nouns: *light, dark, leather, gold, Passover*. Adjectives may be formed from nouns with the addition of a number of suffixes such as the following (perhaps with minor spelling adjustment):

-y: salty, thirsty, mighty, angry
-en: wooden, golden
-ish: childish, foolish, Jewish
-ful: slothful, beautiful, careful, mindful
-less: faithless, fearless, homeless
-worthy: praiseworthy, trustworthy
-ly: heavenly, earthly, disorderly (though be aware that this suffix is more typical of adverbs: §4.3).

The relationship of adjectives to verbs is discussed below (§4.2.3.2).

§4.2.3 Types of Adjective

We may identify a couple of distinctive types of adjective as follows.

§4.2.3.1 Proper Adjectives

Proper adjectives are those based on proper nouns (§2.1.2) and are generally capitalised in English (and often in Greek):

She had an <u>Egyptian</u> servant named Hagar.
Do not pay attention to <u>Jewish</u> myths.
He realised that Paul was a <u>Roman</u> citizen.

§4.2.3.2 Verbal Adjectives

Verbal adjectives are adjectives based on verbal roots and where the force of the related verb is clearly felt in the adjective. There are various ways in which the verbal notion can be turned into an adjective, chiefly in an active sense, a passive sense and a modal (potential) sense.

While many such verbal adjectives are based on participial forms, that these forms have been grammaticalised into adjectives is evident from the fact that (unlike some of their primary verbs) they can often be negated with negative prefixes such as *in-* (*im-, ir-, il-*), *un-* and *dis-*. They can also be preceded by the degree adverbs *more, most, too* and *very* (§4.3.2.2) which are not readily used to modify verbs.

Hebrew and particularly Greek employ adjectives with verbal force.

§4.2.3.2.1 Active Verbal Adjectives

English does have some adjectives with a distinctive adjectival suffix which could be considered as having an active verbal force:

-al: continual, effectual
-ous: prosperous, rebellious, contentious (from *contend*)
-less: ceaseless, thankless
-ant: tolerant, reliant.

English frequently simply uses an adjectival form based on the gerund-participle form of the verb (§3.7.1.3) for this sense:

God keeps his <u>loving</u> covenant with those who love him and obey his commandments.
I have great sorrow and <u>unceasing</u> pain.
You find the hill country of Ephraim too <u>confining</u>.

Rarely verbal adjectives based on the past-participle form (§3.7.1.5) may be used in an active sense:

When sin is full <u>grown</u>, it gives birth to death.
He was in high spirits and very <u>drunk</u>.

§4.2.3.2.2 Passive Verbal Adjectives

The majority of verbal adjectives based on the past-participle form (§3.7.1.5) have a passive force. It is often more difficult to distinguish a passive verbal adjective from a past-participle functioning as part of a compound verb (§3.7.3.2.2.2):

It was made with <u>uncut</u> stones <u>untouched</u> by an iron tool.
You are more <u>blessed</u> than many.
They were too <u>exhausted</u> to escape.

§4.2.3.2.3 Modal Verbal Adjectives

English has the ability to form adjectives from verbal roots containing a **modal** force (§3.3.2) of the verbal idea, i.e. the possibility or potentiality or desirability of the verbal activity. Chief among these are adjectives formed by the addition of the suffix *-able* to the simple form of the verb (perhaps with some minor spelling adjustment). These are generally passive in force, i.e. the meaning is not *able/appropriate to do* but *able/appropriate to be done*:

He took away all his <u>moveable</u> property that he had accumulated.
He will burn up the chaff with <u>inextinguishable</u> fire.
Such sin is <u>punishable</u> by death.

English generally lacks single forms to indicate the quality of the *need* or *obligation* for something to be done or that something is *bound* to happen and most simply expresses such notions with the *to*-infinitive (for active) or *to be* + the past-participle (for passive):

What is <u>to die</u>, let it die, and what is <u>to be eradicated</u>, let it be eradicated. (Zech 11:9)
Everything created by God is good, and nothing is <u>to be rejected</u>. (1 Tim 4:4)
... a worker <u>not needing to be ashamed</u>. (2 Tim 2:15)

Hebrew and Greek employ single forms for the underlined words in the examples above.

§4.2.3.2.4 The Verbal Force of Verbal Adjectives

Verbal adjectives can exercise some of the functions of verbs. They can more readily than many other adjectives take a complement in the form of a *to*-infinitive (though some non-verbal adjectives may also do this):

It is <u>unreasonable to send</u> a prisoner to Rome without specifying the charges against him.

Those <u>unwilling to work</u> will not get to eat.
They were <u>disinclined to hear</u> him further.

Verbal adjectives may not take a direct object. Where a gerund-participle form (*-ing*) is followed by what appears to be an object it is likely to be functioning as a participle or (less frequently) as a gerund (§3.7.3.2.1.2), not as an adjective:

Their actions were <u>provoking</u>. (adjective)
Their actions were <u>provoking</u> him. (participle as part of compound verb)
They sinned by <u>provoking</u> him. (gerund)

However, a verbal adjective can be compounded by being prefixed with an objective element, i.e. a noun that would constitute the object of the related underlying verb:

His appearance was like that of an angel of God, most <u>awe-inspiring</u>.
Those who are <u>self-seeking</u> reject the truth.
Cornelius was a righteous and <u>God-fearing</u> man.

Passive and modal adjectives with a passive force can be linked with an expression of the agent or instrument just like passive verbs (§3.7.2.2):

The judgments <u>given by the Lord</u> are trustworthy.
Yet we did esteem him stricken, <u>smitten of God</u>, and afflicted. (Isa 53:4 KJV; archaic)
There is a remnant, <u>chosen by grace</u>.
If a person commits a sin <u>punishable by death</u> ...
God publicly displayed him at his death as the means of atonement <u>accessible through faith</u>.

§4.2.4 Modifying Adjectives

Adjectives can themselves be modified by adverbs such as *very, quite, never, almost, completely, eternally*:

What you have just said is <u>quite</u> true.
They are <u>almost</u> ready to stone me.

§4.2.5 Adjective Complements

As well as the infinitive complement noted above for some adjectives, some adjectives, as head word of an adjectival phrase, may take a complement in the form of a prepositional phrase:

The tree was good <u>for food.</u>
I am unworthy <u>of all your kindness</u>.
Nothing is too hard <u>for you</u>.

§4.2.6 Degree in Adjectives

Some descriptive adjectives where there can be a gradation in the relative degree of the quality under consideration may exist in three inflectional forms: positive (or simple or no degree), comparative and superlative. Of course many adjectives do not easily lend themselves to the expression of degrees: *sole, absolute, pregnant, dead, eternal*. However, we should not be too hasty to rule out comparative or superlative forms of some such words under some circumstances:

A greater and <u>more perfect</u> tabernacle not made with hands.

Greek has a very similar set of marked degrees in adjectives. Hebrew simply uses the positive adjective which can be understood contextually in a comparative or superlative sense, particularly when accompanied by a prepositional phrase which approximates to *compared with (all)* ...

§4.2.6.1 Positive Degree

The simple or unmarked form of the adjective is the **positive**:

I grew <u>tall</u> like a cedar in Lebanon.
With a <u>strong</u> hand the Lord brought you out of Egypt.
Come to me, all you that are <u>weary</u> and carrying <u>heavy</u> burdens.

§4.2.6.2 Comparative Degree

A **comparative adjective**, typically formed by adding -(*e*)*r* to the positive form of the adjective (perhaps with some minor spelling adjustment), introduces a ranking in relation to one other item or class of items. The object of comparison may be specified after *than*, or left to be inferred from the context:

Urge the <u>younger</u> men to be self-controlled.
What is <u>heavier</u> than lead?
He will boast that he is <u>greater</u> than them all. (Dan 11:37 NLT)

In the final example above, *than* is treated as a preposition and followed by the oblique case *them*. Traditionally *than* after comparatives was treated as a subordinator (§5.3) with ellipsis (gapping) of the rest of the clause and therefore nominative forms were used after it:

I will make of you a nation greater and mightier <u>than they</u> [are]. (Num 14:12; NRSV)

The word *other* can be treated like a comparative:

If anyone preaches to you a gospel <u>other than</u> what you accepted, let them be under God's curse.

§4.2.6.3 Superlative Degree

A **superlative adjective**, typically ending in *-(e)st*, involves a ranking generally of two or more items or classes of item in the purview, though increasingly superlative forms are used for comparisons with only one other item (*the <u>best</u> of the pair*). If there is no limitation of the purview, it is assumed to be universal:

I am the <u>least</u> in my family.
Is not wine the <u>strongest</u>, since it forces people to do these things?
I will cause the <u>heaviest</u> hail to fall that has ever fallen in Egypt.
God exalted him to the <u>highest</u> place.

§4.2.6.4 *More, Most* and *Too*

Many adjectives do not accept, or prefer not to have, the inflectional comparative and superlative suffixes *-(e)r* and *-(e)st*. This is particularly so with longer adjectives and those made of compound elements (*conscientious, hopeful, awesome*), but even some shorter adjectives (*just, evil, sacred*) prefer the auxiliary adverbs *more* (comparative) and *most* (superlative) before the positive form:

Love is <u>more delightful</u> than wine.
You are <u>more evil</u> than all who lived before you.
Gibeon was the <u>most important</u> high place.

This option is available at times also for words which may take the *-(e)r* and *-(e)st* forms, but it is non-standard to use them together (**more greater*) unless for rhetorical effect (the Greek of Eph 3:8 has the equivalent of *leaster*!).

A few common words are irregular in the formation of comparatives and superlatives:

Positive	Comparative	Superlative
good	*better*	*best*
bad	*worse*	*worst*
far	*farther / further*	*farthest / furthest*
much / many	*more*	*most*
little	*littler / less / lesser*	*littlest / least*

A few adjectives with comparative or superlative force effectively lack positive forms: *former, inferior* and forms with *-most*: *in(ner)most, outermost, ut(ter)most, uppermost, foremost, topmost.*

A usage which is closely allied with comparatives is the use of the degree adverb *too* followed by the positive adjective:

I do not concern myself with things too great and too marvellous for me (i.e. great and marvellous in comparison with what I can comprehend).
Is anything too hard for the Lord? (i.e. hard in comparison with his ability to accomplish). This adverbial *too* is not to be confused with *too = also.*

The superlative form with *most* can also be used in an intensifying sense without there being other instances in the purview. It is effectively equivalent to adverbs such as *very, extremely, utterly.* This use is called the **elative**:

Like the sin offering and the guilt offering, it is most holy.
Some from Chloe's household brought a most disturbing report.

Greek inflected superlative forms may have an elative sense.

§4.2.7 Attributive and Predicative Uses of the Adjective

An adjective may function in an attributive or a predicative role.

§4.2.7.1 Attributive Adjectives

An **attributive adjective** is part of the noun phrase it serves to modify; it is on the same 'side' of its clause as its noun. Thus an attributive adjective can be part of the subject, direct or indirect object, possessive form or prepositional phrase. It usually comes before its noun in English, though there is no necessary reason for this to be the case in other languages. With words like *something, anything, nothing,* etc. the adjective is **postpositive** (comes second):

The <u>eternal</u> God grant you his peace.
The Israelites saw the <u>mighty</u> hand of the Lord.
Can anything <u>good</u> come out of Nazareth?

§4.2.7.2 Predicative Adjectives

A predicative use of the adjective is one where the adjective occurs in the predicate but modifies a noun in the subject position of its clause, i.e. noun and adjective are on different sides of the subject / predicate division of the clause (§1.2.4.1). In practice this generally means that in English they will be on either side of a copula (§3.3.2.1) or equative verb such as *be, become, look, feel, seem, appear* etc.

God saw that the light was <u>good</u>.
<u>Just</u> and <u>true</u> are his ways.
I feel <u>confident</u> about you.
The plan seemed <u>right</u>.

Verbs such as *declare, consider* which may take two objects (§3.6) may have a predicative adjective in one of the object positions (though here also we might consider the copula to be implied):

I consider you [to be] <u>godly</u> among this generation.
The unjust judge declares the guilty [to be] <u>innocent</u> and the innocent [to be] <u>guilty</u>.

Most adjectives can be used in either attributive or predicative function with no change of form:

There was a <u>rich</u> man who was dressed in purple. (attributive)
Already you are <u>rich</u>. (predicative)

However, there are some English adjectives that can only be used in the attributive position or only in the predicative position or have a different form in attributive and predicative positions:

The <u>main</u> street of the city is pure gold. (attributive only)
What can <u>mere</u> mortals do to me? (attributive only)
She was <u>asleep</u>. (predicative only)
I was <u>afraid</u>. (predicative only)

The converse uses would be non-standard English:

*The street was <u>main</u>.
*Mortals are <u>mere</u>.

*the <u>asleep</u> woman.
*an <u>afraid</u> person.

These words may be useful diagnostic tools in determining if another adjective is attributive or predicative in context. Substitute the words *main* or *mere* or *asleep* or *afraid* for the adjective you are considering to see if the resulting sentence makes grammatical sense (not necessarily logical sense!). If *main* or *mere* sounds grammatically acceptable but *asleep* or *afraid* does not, the adjective is likely to be attributive. The converse yields a predicative adjective.

Predication with copula + adjective is closely related to predication with a verb:

be healthy = flourish
be asleep = sleep
be afraid = fear
be mindful = remember
be successful = succeed.

The distinction between attributive and predicative uses assumes greater importance in Hebrew and Greek, both of which treat these two uses differently with respect to the use of the definite article. Where English might prefer adjectival predication, Hebrew and Greek may at times prefer to use a verb.

§4.2.8 Substantival Use of the Adjective

Adjectives may be used without any associated noun and may themselves take on the force of a noun, particularly with the addition of a determinative such as the definite article. Such substantival adjectives may constitute the subject, direct or indirect object, possessive form or prepositional complement. Comparative and superlative adjectives, as well as positive, may be used substantivally:

<u>The just</u> shall live by faith.
I had been entrusted with the gospel for <u>the uncircumcised.</u>
<u>The greater</u> shall serve <u>the younger.</u>
They shall all know me, from <u>the least</u> of them to <u>the greatest</u>.

Hebrew and Greek make similar substantival use of adjectives.

§4.2.9 Concord in Adjectives

Adjectives are traditionally said to be in concord with (or to agree with grammatically) the noun they modify or belong closely with. Since there is no inflectional variation in English adjectives to mark such features as number or gender or case, this is not a particularly meaningful observation for English, but it will be useful to remember that a more inflected language like Greek and (to a lesser extent) Hebrew may observe such concord, which helps to bind adjectives and the nouns they modify and disambiguate them from other words. Thus in English *good* is the same whether it goes with *boy*, *soldiers*, *queen*, *lionesses* or *conscience* and whether these noun phrases constitute a subject, direct or indirect object, possessive form or prepositional complement.

§4.2.10 Alternatives to Adjectives

§4.2.10.1 Adjectival Phrases

An adjective can be replaced by a phrase such as a prepositional phrase. Thus a descriptive adjective like *beautiful* could be expressed by *of (great) beauty*; *spiritual* might be *from the Spirit*; *valuable* might be *of (considerable) value*; *everlasting* might be *without end*.

Similarly nouns may be pressed into service as adjectives: the <u>sanctuary</u> shekel; the <u>temple</u> singers; a <u>mountain</u> ravine; <u>covenant</u> mercy. Most nouns can perform this role at least in the attributive position, though more rarely in the predicative position. It makes little difference whether we decide to call these attributive nouns, nouns used as adjectives, or (in some cases) nouns that have grammaticalised into adjectives.

> Languages which have more explicit ways of demonstrating relationships between nouns (e.g. in Hebrew the construct state; in Greek the genitive case) may make more frequent use of nouns where English uses adjectives.

§4.2.10.2 Adjectival Clauses

Some grammars also speak of adjectival clauses, i.e. finite clauses containing a finite verb which effectively perform the function of an attributive adjective. For example, we may say (using an adjective):

God loves a <u>generous</u> person.

We might equally say:

God loves the person <u>who freely gives</u>.

We will call these **relative clauses** and deal with them at §7.2.2.

§4.3 Adverbs

Adverbs modify verbs, adjectives, other adverbs and (what is less commonly recognised) prepositions and (in a limited way) noun phrases. As with adjectives (to which they are closely related), adverbs introduce much finer semantic nuances than is possible without them.

§4.3.1 Adverb Formation

Some adverbs are irreducible lexical items and lack any distinctive formal feature: *so, very, quite, often, soon*. Most adverbs are formed by adding the suffix *-ly* to the corresponding adjective form, including verbal adjectives (§4.2.3.2), perhaps with minor spelling adjustment: *surely, completely, greatly, simply, really, unexpectedly, uncontrollably*. Be aware that some adjectives also end in *-ly*: *holy, lively, ugly, likely, godly*, as do some nouns: *family, assembly*, and some verbs: *supply, multiply*.

§4.3.2 Types of Adverb

In terms of function, adverbs may be of a number of types. These will be closely mirrored by the adverbial clause types treated later (§7.2.3).

Hebrew and Greek have adverbs corresponding to most of the types listed below.

§4.3.2.1 Adverbs of Manner

Adverbs of manner typically tell us *how* the action is performed, such as *well, badly, thus, quickly, skilfully*:

Thus the heavens and the earth were completed.
He looked steadfastly into heaven.
Do not address an older man harshly.

§4.3.2.2 Adverbs of Degree

Adverbs of degree modify constituents of a clause such as a verb, adjective, other adverb, preposition or occasionally even noun phrase with respect to the extent or scope of that constituent. Degree adverbs include *just, only, much, quite, almost, nearly, partly, far, greatly, a little*:

It was getting quite late.
When the four hundred years were nearly up ...
This kingdom will be partly strong and partly brittle.
You are exalted far above all gods.

The adverbs of degree *more, most, too* and *very* (§4.3.2.2) may modify adjectives, adverbs and prepositions but are not readily used with verbs apart from the idiom *the most* (§4.1.3.1):

The boy looked <u>much</u> like a corpse.
<u>Very</u> rarely will anyone die for a righteous person.
An inheritance claimed <u>too</u> soon will not be blessed in the end.
Then they kissed each other and wept together, but David wept <u>the most</u>.

Some adverbs of degree can modify a noun or noun phrase:

In <u>about</u> a year she will have a son.
On the next Sabbath <u>almost</u> the whole town assembled together.
<u>Hardly</u> a day went by without men coming to help.

§4.3.2.3 Adverbs of Place and Direction

Adverbs of place or **direction** locate the activity spatially in absolute or relative terms or in terms of the direction of movement:

We groan <u>inwardly</u> as we wait eagerly for adoption as sons.
He went <u>home</u>, glorifying God.
Then the man led me <u>northward</u> into the outer court.

Many words traditionally treated as adverbs of place (*stand <u>against</u>; put <u>down</u>; hand <u>over</u>; tie <u>up</u>*) are treated differently in this book, as prepositions (§5.1) or elements of prepositional verbs (§3.5).

§4.3.2.4 Adverbs of Time

Adverbs of time or **temporal adverbs** locate the activity in absolute or relative time, such as *still, yet, later, now, eventually, soon*:

Jesus went <u>immediately</u> into the synagogue.
Come <u>soon</u>, Lord Jesus!
<u>Now</u> I know that you fear God.

§4.3.2.5 Adverbs of Frequency

Adverbs of frequency tell us how often the action is performed, including such words as *again, always, ever, frequently, generally, never, occasionally, often, rarely, seldom, sometimes, usually, weekly*:

When you were pagans you were <u>often</u> led astray by speechless idols.
Let your foot be <u>seldom</u> in your neighbour's house.
They will go up <u>annually</u> to worship the King, the Lord who rules over all.

§4.3.2.6 Adverbs of Reason

A small class of adverbs which indicate a rationale for an action may be termed **adverbs of reason**, such as *therefore, thus, accordingly, hence*:

Your obedience is known to all and <u>thus</u> I am rejoicing over you.
Jesus did so with a solemn oath and <u>accordingly</u> has become the guarantee of a better covenant.

§4.3.2.7 Adverbs of Purpose

We might consider a few adverbs to be **adverbs of purpose**, such as *deliberately, accidentally, (un)intentionally*:

But if he strikes him <u>intentionally</u> so that he dies …
Anyone who <u>accidentally</u> killed someone could escape there.

§4.3.2.8 Adverbs of Comparison

Adverbs of comparison indicate that an action or state or quality is like or unlike some point of comparison, including *as, similarly, equally, differently, comparably*:

And <u>similarly</u>, was not Rahab the prostitute also justified by works?
The Lord your God has made you <u>as</u> numerous as the stars of the sky.

§4.3.2.9 Negative Adverbs

The **negators** *not, nowhere* and *never* are traditionally treated as adverbs. These are treated in the section on negation (§6.1).

§4.3.2.10 Other Adverb Categories

A few other adverb categories can be identified (and note that some adverbs could be placed in more than one category). Adverbs of **modality** typically modify a whole clause rather than its verb. They indicate the level of certainty: *perhaps, possibly, probably, doubtless, truly, certainly, assuredly, indeed*. **Evaluative** or **aspectual** adverbs express an evaluation of the speaker on the action: *surprisingly, wondrously, foolishly, providentially*. **Adverbs of sphere** identify the area under discussion or its mode of interpretation: *historically, morally, figuratively*. Other adverbs indicate clausal connections: *so, then, moreover, however, nevertheless, finally*.

§4.3.3 Degree in Adverbs

Adverbs, like adjectives, may have the degrees of **positive**, **comparative** and **superlative**. Traditionally the -*(e)r* and -*(e)st* forms used for comparative and superlative adjectives (*quicker*, *louder*) were considered non-standard when used as adverbs (**She ran quicker*; **He spoke louder*) and are still generally avoided in writing, though increasingly a wider range of such comparative and superlative forms is being used adverbially. A few well accepted adverbial comparative forms in -*(e)r* are *faster*, *sooner*, *longer*:

My days fly by faster than a runner.
No sooner had the large horn become strong than it was broken.
There will no longer be any curse.

In writing, the comparative and superlative forms with the degree adverbs *more* and *most* followed by the positive form of the adverb are generally preferred:

They wither more quickly than grass.
Most importantly, I want to remind you of this.

As with adjectives, there is an **elative** sense of the superlative with *most*, closely analogous to the forms following other degree adverbs such as *very*, *utterly*, *extremely*:

I will most gladly spend and be spent for your sakes.

A few common adverbs, some of which are identical in form to the corresponding adjectives, are irregular in the formation of comparative and superlative forms:

Positive	Comparative	Superlative
well	*better*	*best*
much	*more*	*most / mostly*
little	*less*	*least*

As with adjectives (§4.2.6) Greek marks the three degrees in some adverbs.

§4.3.4 Alternatives to Adverbs

§4.3.4.1 Adverbial Phrases

Many adverbs may be replaced by a phrase, particularly a prepositional phrase with adverbial force:

then = at that time
thus = in this way
therefore = for this reason
how = in what manner, by what means, etc.

In place of these rather general adverbial expressions we could have more specific ones: *the day before yesterday; in vain; under guard; all the time; under no circumstances; in an orderly fashion; in an unworthy manner; without any doubt; without delay; from a long way off.* All of the above are renderings of single adverbs in Hebrew or Greek.

Hebrew, however, does not abound in adverbs, often using an additional verb with adverbial effect:

Hasten and come = Come quickly.
Continued and returned = Continually returned.
To bless I will bless = I will surely bless.

§4.3.4.2 Adverbial Clauses

One of the major types of embedded clause or dependent clause containing a verb is the adverbial clause which effectively fills the slot of an adverb. These are dealt with at §7.2.3.

Exercises for Chapter 4

1. Identify the determinatives in the following:
    a. *Then he gave a loaf of bread, a cake of dates and a cake of raisins to each person in the crowd of Israelites, and all the people went to their homes.*
    b. *He writes the same way in all his letters, speaking in them of these matters. His letters contain some things that are hard to understand, which ignorant and unstable people distort, as they do the other Scriptures, to their own destruction.*
    c. *You people of this generation, listen to what the Lord says.*
    d. *Two people owed money to a certain moneylender. One owed him five hundred denarii, and the other fifty.*

2. Identify the adjectives in the following:
    a. *God made two great lights, the greater light to rule the day and the lesser light to rule the night.*
    b. *What are these remarkable miracles he is performing?*

c. *All those who were in distress or in debt or discontented gathered around him.*

d. *Now the earth was formless and empty.*

e. *Make every effort to be found spotless, blameless and at peace with him.*

f. *The ground was covered with weeds, and the stone wall lay in ruins.*

g. *But whoever does not have them is shortsighted and blind, forgetting that they have been cleansed from their past sins.*

3. Which of the underlined words is a predicative use of the adjective?

   a. *She saw that he was a <u>fine</u> child.*

   b. *No discipline seems <u>pleasant</u> at the time.*

   c. *I will be treated <u>well</u>.*

   d. *Go and see if all is <u>well</u> with your brothers.*

   e. *The Egyptians saw that the woman was very <u>beautiful</u>.*

4. Identify the adverbs in the following:

   a. *Later I returned to Damascus.*

   b. *Paul looked directly at him.*

   c. *He walked faithfully with God.*

   d. *They are almost ready to stone me.*

   e. *The Spirit clearly says that in later times some will abandon the faith.*

5. Parse the underlined words (giving whatever grammatical information is relevant, e.g. part of speech, function, number, degree):

   a. *But the <u>rich</u> should take pride in their humiliation.*

   b. *Very <u>rarely</u> will anyone die for a <u>righteous</u> person.*

   c. *The <u>older</u> will serve the <u>younger</u>.*

   d. *If <u>only</u> a few years remain until the Year of Jubilee, they are to calculate <u>that</u> and pay for their redemption.*

5. Prepositions, Coordinators, Subordinators and Interjections: No Ifs or Buts

Several word classes serve the diverse roles of linkage, of specifying relationships and of expressing emotion.

§5.1 Prepositions

Traditionally prepositions were treated as a rather limited set of generally small words (*to, of, for, by, with, in, on,* etc.) which were then invariably followed by a noun phrase:

On the Sabbath we went outside the city gate to the river.
Without your word no-one will lift hand or foot in all Egypt.
Before the flood, people were eating and drinking.
A Passover like this had not been observed since the days of the judges.

The prepositions then in these examples serve to express the relationship between the following noun phrase and the rest of the clause, indicating such things as place, direction, time, manner and accompanying circumstances. Some prepositions (while capable of more detailed analysis) are most simply treated as a single constituent consisting of more than one word: *out of; in front of; from behind; because of.* Now a larger group of words is recognised as belonging to the same class, including words and phrases that have grammaticalised from other parts of speech: *regardless of; irrespective of; with regard to; for the sake of; with the exception of; in comparison with; in keeping with; for the purpose of.* One group in particular is the class that has developed (or is in process of developing) from the gerund-participle form: *including, excluding, following, concerning, regarding, notwithstanding, according to, judging by, beginning with.*

Be aware that one of the commonest prepositions, *to,* has another function (§3.7.3.2.1.1).

Hebrew and Greek use prepositions in very similar ways to English. Some Hebrew prepositions are attached to their noun complement. Because prepositions cover a wide range of relationships, literal and metaphorical, we cannot assume that the one Greek preposition, for example, covers the same range as one English preposition. We may need to make a distinction, for example between *to* when it relates to motion and when it does not, or between *by* meaning *near* and *by* meaning *through the agency of.*

§5.1.1 Prepositions without Complements

In older grammars any use of a preposition without a following noun phrase was outlawed or treated as something else such as an adverb. A more contemporary way of treating prepositions (as *CGEL*) is to expand their function as well as their number, and to recognise that, like other head words, they may be followed by an empty set (a zero complement):

In this way you are to purge the evil that is <u>within</u>.
I have not seen him <u>since</u>.

Both *within* and *since* may be head of a prepositional phrase, or, as here, may be without complement.

> While some Hebrew and Greek prepositions are restricted to expressions where a noun phrase follows as complement, some can occur independently (usually treated as adverbs when not followed by a complement).

§5.1.2 Prepositions or Adverbs?

Some words previously treated as adverbs are in some contemporary grammars (such as *CGEL*) now regarded as prepositions that never take a complement: *here, there, nearby, downhill, upstairs*. One reason for this is that this class of words is capable of being the complement of a copula (§3.3.2.1) whereas genuine adverbs are not:

The teacher is here.

but not:

**The teacher is usually.*

Some prepositions have become effectively fused to verbs in fixed compounds: *give up, find out, look after* (§3.5).

§5.1.3 Prepositional Complements

Many (but not all) prepositions are capable of taking a (sometimes mandatory) complement in the form of a noun phrase or another preposition + noun phrase. Where the prepositional complement is a personal pronoun or (in writing and more formal style) *who*, English uses inflected accusative (object) forms (§2.4):

If God is for <u>us</u>, who can be against <u>us</u>?
The ground under <u>them</u> split apart.

Why are you talking with <u>her</u>?
I will show mercy on <u>whom</u> I will show mercy.

§5.1.4 Prepositional Phrases as Modifiers or Complements

Prepositional phrases (i.e. preposition ± complement) may serve as modifiers or complements of other constituents. Some prepositional phrases modify nouns in the manner of adjectives, but can introduce greater flexibility:

I am a man <u>under authority</u>.

is roughly equivalent to:

I am a <u>subordinate</u> man.
I hate people <u>with divided loyalties</u>.

is roughly equivalent to:

I hate <u>disloyal</u> people.

Some prepositional phrases modify other constituents in the manner of adverbs but can introduce greater flexibility:

Serve the Lord <u>with great humility</u>.

is roughly equivalent to:

Serve the Lord <u>humbly</u>.
<u>In the end</u> she will wear me out.

is roughly equivalent to:

She will <u>eventually</u> wear me out.

Prepositions and prepositional phrases may form the complement of several elements of the clause:

So Lot stepped <u>outside</u> to talk to them. (verb complement)
They came with the money <u>for the grain</u>. (noun complement)
I will make him a helper suitable <u>for him</u>. (adjective complement)

Both Hebrew and Greek use prepositional phrases as modifiers and complements in ways analogous to English.

§5.1.5 Prepositions with Clause Complement

A number of words identified above as prepositions may take as their complement a non-finite verb (participle or gerund) and so constitute a non-finite clause:

These are the regulations for the burning of offerings.
This was the third time Jesus had shown himself alive to the disciples since being raised from the dead.

Similarly the complement may be in the form of a finite clause:

You had little before I came.
A man ought not to cover his head, since he is the image and glory of God.

While traditionally labelled subordinate conjunctions when introducing finite clauses, these introductory words (even those that only ever take a finite clause complement) are now sometimes considered prepositions (so *CGEL*). Whatever we call them, this group of words, including *than, unless, as, lest, when, if* (conditional), *though* and *although* introduces the types of clause that will be dealt with at §7.2.

§5.1.6 Modifying Prepositional Phrases

Prepositional phrases can themselves be modified by adverbs:

Only in the land of Goshen was there no hail.
All the people will be wholly at your command.
There will be seven years of plenty all through the land of Egypt.

§5.2 Coordinators

Most constituents of a clause can be expanded by coordination with congruent constituents. That is, by linking with the **coordinators** (or coordinating conjunctions) *and, but, or* and *nor* we can add subject to subject, complement to complement, or modifier to modifier:

Then Peter and John placed their hands on the Samaritans. (coordinate subject)
God created the heavens and the earth. (coordinate object)
I will know that you are not spies but honest men. (coordinate predicative complement)
Each one of you should give just as you have decided in your heart, not

reluctantly <u>or under compulsion</u> ... (coordinate modifier in the form of a prepositional phrase)

Coordination may be effected without the use of coordinators. This is more common in strings of three or more coordinated elements where all but the last element may lack a coordinator:

Every three years the fleet returned to port with cargoes of gold, <u>silver, ivory, apes and peacocks</u>.

The coordination of clauses is dealt with at §7.1.

Hebrew and Greek use coordinators in very similar ways to English.

§5.3 Subordinators

CGEL recognises only a limited number of subordinators (traditionally subordinating conjunctions): *that, whether* and *if* (and the latter only when introducing indirect questions):

Examine it to see <u>if</u> it is your son's coat.
It is clear <u>that</u> our Lord is descended from Judah.

A case could be made for including *how* when it is used not to indicate manner, but to introduce a content clause (§7.2.1):

Those who had seen it told them <u>how</u> the man who had been demon-possessed was healed.

Other words traditionally regarded as subordinators are listed under prepositions at §5.1.5.

§5.4 Interjections

One of the major areas of difference between speech and writing, as between different registers of speech, is the area of **interjections**. These words convey in mostly short compass a range of emotional responses to situations, including surprise, fear, delight, approval, disapproval, disgust, pleading, confirmation. Those more likely to be encountered in writing are *oh! alas! please! woe! no! yes! well! ah! aha! ssh! indeed! amen!* Some of these words fulfil other roles. Interjections may stand alone, or be loosely joined to declarations, questions or directives:

At the sound of the trumpet, it says, '<u>Aha</u>!'
<u>Oh no</u>, my master! It was borrowed!

Jacob said, '<u>No, please</u>; if I find favour with you, then accept my gift.'
Then all the people will say, '<u>Amen!</u>'

Exercises for Chapter 5

1. Identify the prepositional phrases (including bare prepositions) in the following:
   a. *Who are these men with you?*
   b. *I give you every seed-bearing plant on the face of the earth and every tree that has fruit with seed in it. They will be yours for food.*
   c. *For three days they travelled in the desert without finding water.*
   d. *From these the nations spread over the earth after the flood.*
   e. *Each of you is to carry a stone on his shoulder, according to the number of the tribes of the Israelites.*
   f. *Go among the whirling wheels underneath the cherubim.*
   g. *On the outside you look righteous to people, but inside you are full of hypocrisy and lawlessness.*

2. Identify the coordinators and subordinators in the following:
   a. *Who told you that you were naked? Have you eaten from the tree that I commanded you not to eat from?*
   b. *I do not know whether he is a sinner.*
   c. *If anyone has material possessions and sees a brother or sister in need but has no pity on them, how can the love of God be in that person?*
   d. *Yet Pharaoh's heart became hard, and he did not listen to them.*
   e. *Hold on to the word of life so that on the day of Christ I will have a reason to boast that I did not run in vain nor labour in vain.*

6. Negation and Interrogation: Why Not?

Both negation (denial) and interrogation (questioning) are variations of an underlying canonical declaration or affirmation (§1.2.4.1.1). Directives (§3.7.3.1.4) may be negated but not turned into questions. These operations deserve separate consideration.

§6.1 Negation

The negation of a statement or directive reverses the polarity, denying or inverting the meaning of the underlying positive clause. Negative statements are those where either one of the constituents or the clause as a whole is negated with a **negator** or negative word *no* or *not* (and the contracted suffix form *-n't*), and derivatives *nor, none, no-one, nothing, never, nowhere*. There are also a few virtual or approximate negatives such as *hardly, barely, scarcely*:

It *hardly* ever leaves him alone.
I *scarcely* know what to do.

§6.1.1 The Scope of Negation: Word- and Phrase-Negation

A negative word can negate most constituents of a clause (subject, predicator, complement, modifier). If the predicator (verb) is negated, the whole clause is negated, though the negation of another key element can have a similar effect. It is not always easy to determine the scope of the negation, particularly where universal words like *all* are involved. A famous example of the subtlety and ambiguity that can be produced by negation is found at the serpent's (mis)quotation of the divine restriction on eating from the fruit of the garden, leaving open the suggestion that the restriction was unduly burdensome:

Has God actually said, 'You are *not* to eat from every tree of the garden'? (Gen 3:1)

Generally the word order (how closely does the negative go with particular words?) will be useful in disambiguation. Hebrew and Greek, no less than English, tend to place the negator in close proximity to the element being negated. In the following, a single constituent (e.g. noun, adjective, adverb, prepositional phrase) is negated:

I saw *no temple* there.
It is the voice of a god, and *not of a man*.

So come and be healed on those days, and <u>not on the Sabbath day</u>.
Tell <u>no-one</u>.
It was <u>not I</u> but God working through me.

Words may be negated with the use of a negative affix, such as the prefixes *a- (an-)*, *in- (im-, il-, ir-)*, *un-*, *dis-*, *non-*, the suffix *-less* and the like. The negative prefix *a-* has been borrowed from Greek (the privative alpha) in words like *agnostic* and *amoral* and used commonly in that language to deprive the unprefixed word of its force or turn a positive word into its polar opposite. Examples of word negation are:

But I am <u>unspiritual</u>.
Nothing is <u>impossible</u> with God.
He fell limp and was <u>lifeless</u>.

§6.1.2 Clause Negation

In **clause negation**, the negator goes closely with the verb. Verbs involving any of the auxiliaries whether used alone or in compound verbs (§3.4) are negated by placing *not* following the auxiliary. For some of these, contracted forms exist in the form of the verbal suffix *-n't*:

I <u>am not</u> an eloquent man.
I <u>am not lying</u>.
I <u>haven't</u> any silver or gold.
I <u>cannot</u>, for I would ruin my inheritance.
It <u>must not be mentioned</u> among you.
I <u>may not have to deal</u> harshly with you.
The Spirit <u>had not</u> yet <u>come</u> upon them.

English does not normally allow a simple negation of a lexical verb just by adding *not* (though this is the norm in Hebrew and Greek). Such a usage is considered archaic in English:

<u>Love not</u> the world (1 John 2:15 KJV).
<u>Think not</u> that I am come to send peace on earth (Matt 10:34 KJV).

To negate what was a simple lexical verb form in a canonical sentence (§1.2.4.1.1) it is more usual to employ a compound construction with a form of the auxiliary *do* (even with the verb *do* itself!). The auxiliary *do* may be a dummy verb in such negation or may have some emphatic force (§3.3.2.2):

He <u>does not lie</u>. (This could be the negative of either *He lies* or the more emphatic *He does lie*.)
You <u>didn't</u> even <u>allow</u> me to kiss my daughters.
The women <u>did not do</u> as the king of Egypt said.

A double negative or two negative words in a sentence (including the negative affixes and virtual negatives) ordinarily suggests a positive (though the effect may be subtly different from having no negatives), as in English the negatives are generally considered to 'cancel each other out':

Whoever does <u>not</u> receive the kingdom of God like a child will <u>never</u> enter it.
I myself will <u>not</u> be <u>disqualified</u>.
Do <u>not</u> regard as <u>inconsequential</u> all the hardship that has befallen us.

This does not apply where the negatives relate to parallel elements and do not separately affect the polarity of the clause:

<u>Neither</u> this man <u>nor</u> his parents sinned.

Be aware that double negatives will not necessarily imply a change of polarity in other languages where a double negative may indicate a strong negative.

Negation can produce further changes from the underlying canonical clause (§1.2.4.1.1). *Some* and its compounds (*something, somebody, somewhere*) may be altered to forms of *any*.

It was early in the morning; there was scarcely <u>any</u> light.
They heard <u>something</u> but did not see <u>anyone</u>.

> Hebrew and Greek, both far less reliant on auxiliaries, negate lexical verbs with a nagator normally preceding the verb.

§6.2 Interrogation

Much of what is said above in relation to negation applies to interrogation (asking questions). Both are transformations of a canonical positive declaration (§1.2.4.1.1). Questions are of two basic types — **open questions,** to which there could be any number of answers, and **closed questions** that ask for confirmation or denial of a proposition. In either case, the question can be a genuine question, or a rhetorical device.

§6.2.1 Open Questions

In an **open question**, a questioner seeks a piece of information (or rarely two or more pieces of information within the same clause) using a *wh-* word:

who (*whom, whose*)? *what? which? when? where? why?* or *how?* (okay, that last one sneaked into the *wh-* group). Hebrew and Greek have equivalents for these *wh-* words. The question word is a placeholder for the missing term in a canonical statement:

<u>Whose</u> daughter are you? (You are the daughter of X.)
<u>Who</u> do people say that I am? (People say that I am X.)
<u>When</u> will you understand? (You will understand at x time.)
By <u>what</u> authority are you doing all these things? (You are doing these things by x authority.)
<u>How</u> will they hear without a preacher? (They will hear without a preacher by x means. A rhetorical question; the value of x is assumed to be nil.)

The actual response could be given as the whole clause with the missing term supplied, e.g. (from the first example above):

I am Bethuel's daughter.

Or it could assume the rest of the information from the question and just supply the missing term: *Bethuel's.* Hebrew and Greek do the former more commonly than English. Occasionally the questioner may include within the question some suggestions for answers to the specific interrogative element (thus nudging in the direction of a closed question if the suggested responses are felt to be exclusive):

Who sinned, <u>this man, or his parents,</u> that he should be born blind?
What would you prefer — <u>that I came to you with a rod of discipline, or with love and a spirit of gentleness</u>?

§6.2.2 Closed Questions

The other type of question is the **closed question** (a *yes / no* question) where the questioner seeks to ascertain the truth or falsehood of a statement. Languages employ a variety of strategies for formulating such questions. There are both unmarked and marked questions of this type.

§6.2.2.1 Unmarked Closed Questions

A closed question may be asked without any grammatical indication that it is a question. The question may be indicated in speech by voice intonation and/or other contextual features (such as facial expression) and in writing simply by a question mark:

You are well?
So you want to go with this man?

Since Hebrew and Greek may also employ grammatically unmarked questions (and the question mark is a late addition to Greek texts), we are uncertain whether some sentences in the Bible are intended as statements or questions. Compare:

My Father's house has many rooms; if that were not so, would I have told you that I am going there to prepare a place for you? (John 14:2 NIV2011)

with:

There are many dwelling places in my Father's house. Otherwise, I would have told you, because I am going away to make ready a place for you (John 14:2 NET).

§6.2.2.2 Marked Closed Questions

More commonly closed questions are marked. In English, clauses containing an auxiliary verb are turned into questions by an inversion of the canonical (§1.2.4.1.1) word order of subject and auxiliary verb:

Shall I hide it?
Must you rescue him?
Are they descendants of Abraham?
Has he ever said ...?

For simple lexical verbs, and normally for the verbs *do* and *have* when used as lexical verbs, it is necessary to supply a form of the auxiliary *do* if there is no auxiliary in the canonical (§1.2.4.1.1) statement:

Did any gods rescue Samaria from my power?
Do you want to go with this man?
Did I do any wrong?
Do I still have sons in my womb that they may become your husbands? (Ruth 1:11 NRSV)

Note that the treatment of the verb *have* without an auxiliary in questions is now confined to literary contexts and is otherwise considered archaic:
Have I any pleasure at all that the wicked should die? (Ezek 18:23 KJV)

§6.2.2.2.1 Neutral and Biased Closed Questions

A closed question can be neutral or biased, i.e. loaded with an expectation of a *yes* or *no* answer.

§6.2.2.2.1.1 Neutral Closed Questions

Neutral questions have no leaning towards either a positive or a negative response and this is sometimes reinforced with a formula that expresses the alternatives (with *or*):

Is this where the seer is?
Should I attack Ramoth Gilead or not?

§6.2.2.2.1.2 Biased Closed Questions

Biased questions have a built-in expectation of either a positive or a negative answer (sometimes with a modal force that the answer *should* be one or the other (from the speaker's perspective), though the actual anticipated response may be assumed to be otherwise. Questions expecting a positive response include a negator in English (as in Hebrew and Greek):

Do people <u>not</u> get back up when they fall down?
Are there <u>not</u> twelve hours in a day?
Wo<u>n't</u> you answer?
Though you have ears, ca<u>n't</u> you hear?

Questions expecting a *yes* answer may in English take the form of a confirmatory question, i.e. a complete statement of the answer expected, followed by a truncated question or interrogative tag seeking confirmation (auxiliary verb + negator + pronoun subject in interrogative order):

It's just a little place, <u>isn't it</u>?

Questions expecting a negative answer (or expecting that the answer *should* be *no*) can take the same form in English (and Hebrew) as neutral questions, so context is needed to determine the bias (if any) of the question:

Have you ever seen a man give birth?
Can you discover the perfection of the Almighty?
Was Paul crucified for you?

Questions expecting a *no* answer may in English take the form of a confirmatory question, i.e. a complete statement, followed by an interrogative tag (auxiliary verb + pronoun subject in interrogative order):

I have not taken advantage of you, have I?
All do not speak in tongues, do they?

While closed questions grammatically anticipate a simple confirmation or denial, the actual response can be quite varied, with perhaps an evasion, or extraneous information supplied, or a question directed back to the interlocutor. Sometimes a measure of irony or sarcasm can play with the polarity of the bias:

You aren't one of his disciples too, are you?

Just as happens in negation, interrogation may cause some other changes, such as the shift from forms of *some-* to forms of *any-*:

Why didn't <u>anyone</u> answer when I called?
Do we still have <u>any</u> share in the inheritance of our father's estate?

Hebrew and Greek do not regularly use the interrogative tag or distinguish *some-* forms from *any-* forms, but otherwise employ similar strategies for formulating closed questions.

Exercises for Chapter 6

1. Give the underlying canonical form (active rather than passive; positive rather than negative) of the following. Use X for a placeholder where necessary:
    a. *No-one was found who was worthy to open the scroll or to look into it.*
    b. *My time has not yet come.*
    c. *I was not a burden to anyone.*
    d. *Is there no sword or spear here at your disposal?*
    e. *What does this mean?*
    f. *Who does not know such things as these?*
    g. *Where have you laid him?*
    h. *Why do you stand here?*

2. Identify the open and closed questions in the following. For closed questions indicate whether the question is neutral or biased and what the bias is:
    a. *Can anyone teach God knowledge, since he judges those that are on high?*
    b. *If others have this right of support from you, shouldn't we have it all the more?*
    c. *How long will you refuse to humble yourself before me?*
    d. *Do people bring in a lamp to put it under a bowl or a bed?*

e. *Tell us, when will these things happen?*

f. *Are you the man who spoke to my wife?*

g. *But now be so kind as to look at me. Would I lie to your face?*

h. *The rivers of Damascus, the Abana and Pharpar, are better than any of the waters of Israel! Could I not wash in them and be healed?*

7. When One Clause Just Isn't Enough

§7.1 Clause Coordination

Like words and phrases (§5.2) clauses may be coordinated. Though in writing we conventionally regard a sentence as concluding with a full stop (period) or question mark or exclamation mark, the boundaries of what constitutes a sentence are fuzzier than we may realise. As well as coordinating clauses within a sentence, the coordinators *and, but, or, nor* and *yet* may introduce independent sentences loosely connected with the preceding sentences, so it is more a convention of writing to break them up the way we do.

Clauses are of two basic types: the **independent clause**, a finite clause (§3.7.3.1) which is capable of forming a sentence alone, or with other clauses, and the **dependent clause** which is only capable of being embedded or nested within another clause. Independent clauses may be coordinated with each other, as may congruent dependent clauses (e.g. content clause + content clause: §7.2.1; or conditional protasis + conditional protasis: §7.2.3.8). The **coordinate clauses** are underlined in the following:

The Lord God caused a deep sleep to fall upon the man, <u>and he slept</u>.
(coordinate independent clause)
They will kill me, <u>but they will let you live</u>. (coordinate independent clause)
I will not break my covenant <u>nor will I go back on my promise</u>. (coordinate independent clause)
Ravens have no storeroom or barn, <u>yet God feeds them</u>. (coordinate independent clause)
You yourself know how I have served you, <u>and how your livestock has fared with me</u>. (coordinate dependent clause)
If you have done foolishly <u>or if you have planned evil</u>, put your hand over your mouth. (coordinate dependent clause)

As with coordination of words and phrases, clause coordination may be effected without the use of coordinators. This is more common in strings of three or more clauses where all but the last clause may lack a coordinator:

When the woman saw that the tree produced fruit that was good for food, <u>was attractive to the eye, and was desirable for making one wise</u>, she took some of its fruit and ate it.

Within a sentence consisting of two or more coordinate clauses, parallel constituents may be gapped in one or other clause, particularly the subject where both clauses have the same subject:

I sought him, but did not find him. (subject is gapped in second clause)
Their competing thoughts will either accuse or excuse them. (object is gapped in first clause and subject in second)

Elements of a compound verb or less commonly the whole verb may be gapped in a coordinate clause:

They will eat, but not be satisfied.
You will go to the right and we to the left.

We could distinguish between coordination and **supplementation**. Supplementation is the adding of material that is not strictly coordinate with the rest of the sentence to which it is attached. In English this is frequently marked with the long dash:

But in my judgment, she is happier if she remains as she is — and I think that I too have the Spirit of God!
They will undergo the punishment of eternal destruction when he comes to be glorified among his saints on that day among all who have believed — and you have believed our testimony.

§7.2 Embedded or Subordinate Clauses

A high proportion of sentences in written English include clauses which effectively fill constituent slots within another clause, i.e. one clause is grammatically subordinate to the other, or embedded (nested) within it (which may occur at the beginning, within, or at the end of the host clause). The host clause is generally called the main clause, though it would be more accurate to call it the **matrix clause**, as an embedded clause may be nested within a clause which is itself nested within another clause:

I will make your offspring like the dust of the earth so that if one can count the dust of the earth, your offspring also can be counted.

Here we have a matrix clause:

I will make your offspring like the dust of the earth,

in which is embedded the clause:

so that ... your offspring also can be counted

in which is embedded the clause:

if one can count the dust of the earth.

Embedded clauses may be either non-finite (with a non-finite verb form — infinitive, gerund or participle) — or finite. Non-finite clauses are not so easily employed where the subject of the embedded clause is different from the subject of the matrix clause. There are a number of distinct types of embedded clause which we may broadly identify as those filling the noun slot, the adjective slot and the adverb slot of the matrix clause.

§7.2.1 Content or Noun Clauses

A major type of embedded clause is the **content clause** or **noun clause**, including the clause of reported (indirect) speech, embedded directives and embedded questions. A content clause most commonly serves as the complement of a verb, noun or adjective particularly those connected with speech, thought, perception, fear etc. Verbs of saying, thinking, perceiving etc. may take as their direct object a simple noun, a longer phrase, a non-finite clause or a finite clause to indicate the content of what is said, thought, etc.

A content clause may be expressed by a non-finite clause:

I heard <u>someone speaking to me</u>. (participial clause)
This same Jesus who has been taken up from you into heaven will come back in the same way you saw <u>him go into heaven</u>. (infinitive-clause)

A finite content clause may be introduced by the subordinator *that* or less commonly *how* (§5.3). The following content clauses are verbal complements:

God saw <u>that the light was good</u>.
Jacob learned <u>that there was grain in Egypt</u>.
I fear <u>that harm might come to him</u>.
He told them <u>how Saul on his journey had seen the Lord</u>.

The following content clauses are complements of a noun or adjective:

There is a rumour <u>that you are going to become their king</u>. (complement of noun)
By this we are aware <u>that God resides in us</u>. (complement of adjective)

That (or *how*) is not indispensible in a content clause. English, along with Hebrew and Greek, allows **paratactic** or **asyndetic** content clauses where the content clause is simply embedded without grammatical marker:

I fear <u>harm might come to him</u>.
I know <u>you will not hold me innocent</u>.

The content of speech, after verbs of saying, telling, answering etc. may be given as either **direct speech** or **indirect speech**. The preference for direct speech (the quoted words) is a common stylistic feature of both the Hebrew and Greek of the Bible. Where speech is reported indirectly, the pronouns and tenses might be changed from the underlying direct statement, to reflect the perspective of the speaker (or narrator) of the report rather than the original speaker where these are different:

She ran in and announced <u>that Peter was standing at the gate</u>.
They told us <u>that they had seen a vision of angels who said that he was alive</u>.

Note the two layers of embedding in the second example. Using direct speech, this would be:

They told us, 'We have <u>seen a vision of angels who said, "He is alive"</u>'.

We cannot assume that other languages will necessarily adopt precisely the same strategy as English with regard to the form of content clauses, including indirect speech. Tenses in particular may be unaltered from the underlying direct discourse.

§7.2.1.1 Embedded Directive Clauses

A subcategory of the content clause is the **embedded directive clause**. The content of commands, pleas and other directives may be embedded in a subordinate clause which is a complement of a verb or noun of commanding, pleading, praying etc. A non-finite clause is typically formed with a *to*-infinitive:

He ordered him <u>to be quiet</u>.
Did I not tell you <u>not to harm the boy</u>?

A finite embedded directive is typically introduced by *that* + the subjunctive mood (§3.7.3.1.3) or a modal auxiliary such as *may* or *might*:

Pray <u>that it may not be in winter</u>. (complement of verb)
Caesar Augustus issued a decree <u>that all the world should be taxed</u>. (complement of noun)
It is necessary <u>that this high priest should also have something to offer</u>. (complement of adjective)

§7.2.1.2 Embedded Question Clauses

The content of both open and closed questions (§6.2.1-2) may similarly be embedded within longer sentences. The **embedded** (or indirect) **question** may occupy the slot of the object of a verb of asking, knowing, perceiving, revealing, wondering etc. or form the complement of other parts of speech. For some verbs, such as *ask*, this may mean a double object (§3.6). Be aware that *ask* also has the function of introducing polite directives (§7.2.1.1).

Open embedded questions retain the interrogative element (*who, what, where,* etc.: §6.2.1) at the beginning of the embedded clause:

David asked the Lord <u>what he should do</u>. (complement of verb)
Explain <u>how this wicked thing happened</u>. (complement of verb)
He was not aware <u>when she lay down</u>. (complement of adjective)

Such embedded clauses with a *wh-* word are not to be confused with relative clauses which are also introduced by the *wh-* group of words (§7.2.2).

Closed embedded questions are generally introduced in English by *whether* or *if*:

Go, inquire of Baalzebub <u>whether I will recover from this sickness</u>.
(complement of verb)
Test the spirits to determine <u>if they are from God</u>. (complement of verb)
The king of Babylon was uncertain <u>whether to attack Jerusalem or Rabbah</u>.
(complement of adjective)

These are not to be confused with conditional clauses which may also begin with *if* and more rarely *whether* (§7.2.3.8).

Note that an embedded (indirect) question may represent a modification of the canonical (§1.2.4.1.1) direct question in several respects. The word order may be slightly different and there may no longer be need to employ auxiliaries. The tense and person forms may be varied so as to reflect the perspective of the speaker (or narrator) of the reported question rather than the original asker (if different). Similarly words which indicate proximity or distance in space or time (*here, there, this, that, now, then*) may be altered:

Explain <u>how this wicked thing happened.</u>

has as its underlying direct question:

How did this wicked thing happen?
Cornelius asked <u>whether Simon Peter was staying there</u>.

has as its underlying direct question:

Is Simon Peter staying here?

We cannot assume that other languages will necessarily adopt precisely the same strategy as English in this regard. Tenses in particular may be unaltered from the underlying direct question. In Hebrew and in Greek it is not always easy to tell whether a question is intended to be understood as direct or embedded and it will make little difference how one translates such passages:

Now when Pilate heard this, he asked whether the man was a Galilean (Luke 23:6 NET)

'Oh, is he a Galilean?' Pilate asked. (Luke 23:6 NLT).

Occasionally the subjunctive verb form is found in embedded questions in English (§3.7.3.1.3). This usage is now considered literary or archaic.

When Pilate heard of Galilee, he asked whether the man <u>were</u> a Galilaean (Luke 23:6 KJV).

§7.2.2 Relative or Adjectival Clauses

The adjective constituent slot of a clause can be filled by a longer phrase or by a clause. Consider the following:

I saw a <u>heavenly</u> messenger. (adjective)
I saw a messenger <u>from heaven.</u> (prepositional phrase)
I saw a messenger <u>coming from heaven.</u> (non-finite clause)
I saw a messenger <u>who came from heaven</u>. (finite clause)

Greek particularly is capable of forming complex adjectives for which English has no simple adjective equivalent, e.g. *not-made-with-hands, brother/sister-loving, seeking-dishonest-gain.* These will need to be rendered into English by phases or clauses.

Prepositional phrases, which can fill the adjective slot, are dealt with at §5.1.3-4.

Non-finite clauses with an adjectival role typically have a participle as their non-finite verb. We may call these non-finite **relative clauses** as the clause relates to a word in the matrix clause, i.e. the subject of the participle is also a constituent in the matrix clause:

David was the one <u>leading them out to battle</u>. (*David* is the subject of the matrix clause and of the participle.)

They could not conquer the people <u>living in the coastal plain</u>. (*People* is the object of the matrix clause and subject of the participle.)
They brought the sick and those <u>troubled by unclean spirits</u>. (*Those* is the object of the matrix clause and subject of the participle.)

Another non-finite relative clause is formed with the *to*-infinitive:

All authority is his, not only in this age, but in the age <u>to come</u>.
These are the bowls <u>to be used in pouring out offerings</u>.

The **relative clause** may also be expressed as a finite clause. Consider the sentence:

He saw his brothers who were outside.

The matrix clause is: *He saw his brothers.* The relative clause is: *who were outside,* where the relative pronoun *who* substitutes for *his brothers.* There is then one constituent common to both clauses. *His brothers* is the object of the first clause and (represented by the relative pronoun) the subject of the second. The word or phrase to which the relative pronoun refers (*his brothers*) is called its **antecedent**. The relative pronoun shares some features of its antecedent. If the antecedent is masculine and singular, the relative pronoun will also be said to share these attributes. In practice this makes little difference in English as we do not mark gender or number in relative pronouns. We do, however, mark a distinction between personal (*who*) and impersonal (*which*), though *that* can serve for either:

Those <u>who</u> love your law are completely secure.
This is the day <u>which</u> the Lord has made.
The people <u>that</u> walked in darkness have seen a great light.

Be aware that *which* and *that* have other functions.

The case (§2.3.3) of the relative pronoun is not as a rule taken from its antecedent, but from its function in its own (embedded) clause. Written or more formal English does mark a distinction in the case of the relative pronoun *who*. Where the relative pronoun is a direct or indirect object, or in a prepositional phrase, the form *whom* is generally used in written English. In the sentence:

The disciple whom Jesus loved was reclining next to him.

we have two clauses (because two separate verbs). The underlying independent clauses would be:

The disciple was reclining next to Jesus.
Jesus loved the disciple.

Here *the disciple* is subject of the first clause, but direct object of the second, hence the oblique (non-subject) form *whom* is used. The form *whose* is used when the relative word is genitive or possessive:

For there stood by me this night the angel of God, <u>whose</u> I am, and whom I serve.

A relative pronoun can also be the complement of a prepositional phrase:
Take up the shield of faith <u>with which</u> you can extinguish all the flaming darts of the evil one.
This happened to many others, some <u>of whom</u> were beaten, others killed.

Logically, relative clauses can be either restrictive or non-restrictive. The restrictive type limits the reference of the antecedent by the criteria in the relative clause:

All the people <u>who were descended from Jacob</u> numbered seventy.

The non-restrictive relative clause adds information about the referent but does not limit it:

He died an old man <u>who had lived a full life</u>.

Relative pronouns are not an indispensible component of a relative clause. English, along with Hebrew and Greek, allows **paratactic** or **asyndetic** relative clauses where the relative clause is simply embedded without grammatical marker:
This is the day <u>the Lord has made</u>.
The disciple <u>Jesus loved</u> was reclining next to him.
The one <u>I kiss</u> is the man.

Sometimes the antecedent can be dispensed with; the relative pronoun suffices to represent the term common to both clauses. This is particularly so with the indefinite relative forms *whoever, whatever*:
<u>Whoever</u> finds me will kill me.
Eat <u>whatever</u> is served without asking questions.

Hebrew and Greek use relative clauses in very similar ways to English.

§7.2.3 Adverbial Clauses

The modifier function of an adverb in a clause can similarly be filled by an **adverbial clause**, either non-finite (employing a participle or gerund) or finite (employing a finite verb). Older grammars preferred to call non-finite clauses phrases. Compare the following:

A certain man drew his bow and <u>randomly</u> struck the king of Israel. (adverb)
A certain man drew his bow and <u>not realising it</u> struck the king of Israel. (non-finite participial clause)
A certain man drew his bow and <u>without targeting him</u> struck the king of Israel. (non-finite gerund-clause)
A certain man drew his bow and, <u>though he had not aimed to do so</u>, struck the king of Israel. (finite adverbial clause)

Adverbial clauses can be of several types, broadly corresponding to the several types of adverb, including manner, place and direction, temporal, frequency, reason, purpose, result, conditional, concessive and comparison.

§7.2.3.1 Manner Clauses

An adverbial **manner clause** further expands the potential of adverbs of manner (§4.3.2.1).

Non-finite manner clauses are formed with participles or gerunds:

God showed how much he loved us <u>by sending his one and only Son into the world</u>. (gerund-clause)
From there he expanded his territory to Assyria, <u>building the cities of Nineveh, Rehoboth-ir and Calah</u>. (participial clause)
I brought glory to you here on earth <u>by completing the work</u> you gave me to do. (gerund-clause)
I charge you to obey this command <u>without wavering</u>. (gerund-clause)

Finite manner clauses are typically introduced by *how*, *as* and *the way*:

He did it <u>how he was shown</u>.
So I prophesied <u>as I was commanded</u>.
'You don't want to kill me <u>the way you killed the Egyptian</u>, do you?'

§7.2.3.2 Place and Direction Clauses

An **adverbial clause of place** or **direction** further expands the potential of expressions of place or direction (§4.3.2.3). Such are typically introduced by *where, wherever, anywhere, everywhere*:

Where your treasure is, there your heart will be also.
These follow the Lamb wherever he goes.
He did this everywhere you went until you came to this place.

§7.2.3.3 Temporal Clauses

An adverbial clause of time or **temporal clause** further expands the potential of adverbial time expressions (§4.3.2.4). Such clauses locate the action of the matrix clause in real or relative time.

Non-finite temporal clauses may be formed with participles (§3.7.3.2.2) or gerunds (§3.7.3.2.1.2) introduced by such words as *since, after, before*:

Having been freed from sin, you became slaves to righteousness. (participial clause)
Returning home, he calls his friends and neighbours. (participial clause)
After waiting another seven days, Noah released the dove again. (gerund-clause)
This was now the third time Jesus had shown himself alive to the disciples since being raised from the dead. (gerund-clause)

Finite temporal clauses are typically introduced by *when, while, as, as long as, as soon as, until, till, before, after* and *since*:

If they do this when the wood is green, what will happen when it is dry?
Twenty years have passed since I left this money in trust.
In the evening, after the sun had set, they brought to him all who were sick and demon-possessed.
Hebrew women give birth before the midwife comes to them.
The sun is darkened as soon as it rises.

§7.2.3.4 Frequency Clauses

An adverbial **frequency clause** further expands the potential of adverbs expressing frequency (§4.3.2.5).

Non-finite frequency clauses are typically formed with participles or gerunds introduced by such words as *when(ever)*:

When reviled, we bless; when persecuted, we endure.
When entering a town or village, find out who is worthy there.

Finite frequency clauses are typically introduced by *whenever, as often as, each time, every time*:

Whenever you pray, go into your room, shut the door, and pray to your Father in secret.
Do this, every time you drink it, in remembrance of me.
As often as the Philistines marched out, David achieved more success than all of Saul's servants.

§7.2.3.5 Reason Clauses

An adverbial **reason clause** further expands the potential of adverbs and adverbial phrases of reason (§4.3.2.6). An adverbial clause of reason gives a rationale for the matrix clause.

A non-finite reason clause is typically formed with a participle, or a gerund introduced by *because of*:

We rejoice in sufferings, knowing that suffering produces endurance.
(participial clause)
If a person who is ritually unclean because of touching a dead body ...
(gerund-clause)

A finite reason clause is typically introduced by *because, for* or *since*:

For what can be known about God is plain to them, because God has shown it to them.
Since death came through a human being, the resurrection of the dead has also come through a human being.

Reason clauses, particularly those introduced by *for*, can have a couple of different functions. They can give the reason for the content of the matrix (or preceding) clause:

Each of you must give as you have determined, not reluctantly or under compulsion, for God loves a cheerful giver.

Or they may introduce the reason for the inclusion of the information. In this role, *for* often introduces a grammatically independent clause at the sentence level:

Or do you not know, brothers and sisters (for I am speaking to those who know the law), that the law is lord over people as long as they live?

§7.2.3.6 Purpose Clauses

A **purpose** or **final clause** introduces the stated intention or objective prompting the action of the matrix clause. It can be realised by an adverb, an adverbial phrase, a non-finite clause or a finite clause. Consider the following:

He delivered them purposefully. (adverb)
He delivered them for the sake of his glory. (adverbial prepositional phrase)
He delivered them to reveal his glory. (infinitive-clause)
He delivered them that he might reveal his glory. (finite clause)

Non-finite purpose clauses typically have a *to*-infinitive which may be introduced by *in order* or *so as*:

You have come to see if our land is vulnerable.
They were hiring advisers to oppose them, so as to frustrate their plans.

Finite positive purpose clauses are typically introduced by *that, in order that, so (that)*. Be aware that *that* and *so that* can introduce either a purpose or a result clause (§7.2.3.7) and *that* can also introduce a content clause and a relative clause:

I have chosen him so that he will direct his sons and their families to keep the way of the Lord. (purpose clause)
Locusts will cover the land so that you will not be able to see the ground. (result clause)
I had no idea that they were planning to kill me! (content clause)

Negative purpose clauses may be introduced by *lest* or by negation of a *that, in order that* or *so that* clause:

Don't sin any more, lest anything worse happen to you.
May I be fully committed to your statutes, so that I might not be ashamed.

§7.2.3.7 Result Clauses

A **result clause** introduces the result or consequence of the action of the matrix clause.

Non-finite result clauses may be formed in a variety of ways, such as with a participle, perhaps introduced by *so* or *thus*, or a *to*-infinitive which may be introduced by *so as*:

He did this to create in himself one new man out of two, <u>thus making peace</u>.
For God is not unjust <u>so as to forget your work</u>.

Finite result clauses are typically introduced by *that, such that, so (that), with the result that*. The words *such* or *so* can be incorporated into the matrix clause. Be aware that some of these words can introduce other clause types, particularly purpose clauses (§7.2.3.6). While purpose and result may happily coincide, there is of course a logical distinction between intention and outcome. Some result clauses are:

For God so loved the world, <u>that he gave his only Son</u>.
What are human beings <u>that you pay attention to them</u>?
He was indeed so ill <u>that he nearly died</u>.
Who sinned, <u>such that this man was born blind</u>?

§7.2.3.8 Conditional Clauses

A **conditional clause** introduces a potential or counterfactual situation. It might be thought of as filling the slot of an adverb such as *conditionally, provisionally*, or a phrase such as *under certain circumstances*.

Non-finite conditional clauses may be formed in a variety of ways, e.g. with a participle introduced by *if* or (for double conditions) *whether* or (for negative conditions) by *except by* + gerund:

<u>If looking for me</u>, let these men go.
<u>If shaken</u> they fall into the mouth of the eater.
<u>Whether born in your household or bought with your money</u>, they must be circumcised.
Anyone who competes as an athlete does not receive the victor's crown <u>except by competing according to the rules</u>.

Typical finite conditional clauses are introduced by *(even) if, provided (that), supposing*, and for negative conditions *unless*. The condition to be met (the *if* clause) is called the **protasis**. The matrix clause, the **apodosis**, may be a statement, a directive or a question. Its truth or validity or relevance is contingent on the outcome of the condition in the protasis. Protasis and apodosis may occur in either order. The protasis is typically introduced by *if*, or more rarely by variants such as *provided (that), supposing*:

If you worship me, it will all be yours.
If you are the Son of God, tell this stone to become bread.
It is fine to be zealous, provided the purpose is good.

A negative protasis may be introduced by *unless*:

I will not let you go unless you bless me.

Some conditions are more hypothetical or remote or unreal, in that the condition cannot be met or is considered unlikely to be met. English may use subjunctive (§3.7.3.1.3) and modal verb forms (§3.3.2) for such conditions, both in the protasis and the apodosis:

Now if he were on earth, he would not be a priest.
Even if they were to hide on the top of Mount Carmel, I would hunt them down and take them from there.
Even supposing I were to ask you, would you respond?
Lord, if you had been here, my brother would not have died.

In a construction now becoming obsolete, a subjunctive mood or modal verb + subject may introduce a protasis without *if* or equivalent:

Were I to proclaim and tell of them, they would be more than can be counted.
But should you not obey the voice of the Lord your God, then all these curses will come upon you.

A double condition (itemising more than one potentiality) may be in the form *whether … or …*:

Whether we live or die, we belong to the Lord.

Be aware that embedded or indirect questions may also begin with *if* or *whether* (§7.2.1.2).

Occasionally, a protasis may occur without an apodosis, leaving the consequence of the fulfilment of the condition unstated for rhetorical effect:

And if they don't believe me or pay attention to me, but say, 'The Lord hasn't appeared to you'?

§7.2.3.9 Concessive Clauses

A **concessive clause** introduces a factor that is somewhat at odds with the expectation created by the rest of the statement. It fills out the role of an adverb or adverbial phrase. Consider the following:

The servants went out and rounded up everyone they laid eyes on, good and bad, <u>indiscriminately</u>. (adverb)
The servants went out and rounded up everyone they laid eyes on, good and bad, <u>without discrimination</u>. (adverbial prepositional phrase)
The servants went out and rounded up everyone they laid eyes on, good and bad, <u>despite their being of diverse character</u>. (gerund-clause)
The servants went out and rounded up everyone they laid eyes on, good and bad, <u>although they were of diverse character</u>. (finite clause)

A non-finite concessive clause may be formed with *although* or *though* + participle:

<u>Though seeing</u>, they do not see.
The men of Ephraim, <u>though armed with bows</u>, turned back on the day of battle.
What if God, <u>although choosing to show his wrath and make his power known</u>, bore with great patience the objects of his wrath?

A finite concessive clause is typically introduced by *although*, *(even) though* or *while*. It may come before or after the matrix clause:

<u>Though I was blind</u>, now I see.
<u>Although they fast</u>, I do not hear their cry.
He found no chance to repent, <u>even though he sought the blessing with tears</u>.
<u>While I have many other things to write to you</u>, I do not want to do so with paper and ink.

Be aware that *while* also introduces temporal clauses (§7.2.3.3).

§7.2.3.10 Comparison Clauses

A **comparison clause** introduces a point of comparison with the matrix clause. Comparisons can be expressed by an adverb, an adverbial phrase, a non-finite clause or a finite clause. Comparison clauses are typically introduced by such words as *as, as if, as though, like* and *(rather) than*:

It is <u>like seeing the face of God</u>. (gerund-clause)
They will be condemned for enjoying evil rather <u>than believing the truth</u>. (gerund-clause)
The men of Ephraim, <u>though armed with bows</u>, turned back on the day of battle. (participial clause)
I wish that everyone was <u>as I am</u>. (finite clause)
Why do you stare at us <u>as if we had made this man walk by our own power or</u>

piety? (finite clause)
Therefore we are ambassadors for Christ, <u>as though God were making his plea through us</u>. (finite clause)
It will be <u>like it is piled up to heaven</u>. (finite clause)

A comparative adjective or adverb (§4.2.6.2, §4.3.3), as well as taking a comparison phrase, may take a non-finite or finite comparison clause as its complement:

I could have no greater joy <u>than to hear</u> that my children are following the truth. (infinitive-clause)
My punishment is more <u>than I can bear</u>. (finite clause)
Do not think more highly of yourself <u>than you ought to think</u>. (finite clause)

Exercises for Chapter 7

1. Identify the non-finite clauses (with infinitive, gerund or participle) and indicate their function (content, relative or adverbial and if possible what type of adverbial):
    a. *They asked him to show them a sign from heaven.*
    b. *I glorified you on earth by finishing the work you gave me to do.*
    c. *He knows your coming and your going.*
    d. *They routed those living in the valleys.*
    e. *Having been warned in a dream not to go back to Herod, they returned to their country by another route.*

2. Identify the finite embedded clauses (i.e. with finite verb) and indicate their type:
    a. *I know that you have done this with a clear conscience.*
    b. *Find out what makes him so strong and how we can subdue him.*
    c. *The Lord put a mark on Cain, so that no one who came upon him would kill him.*
    d. *They multiplied and grew exceedingly strong, so that the land was filled with them.*
    e. *I am told that he is very cunning.*
    f. *This is how I will find out if you are honest men.*
    g. *Were I to count them, they would outnumber the grains of sand.*

h. *I know that you fear God, since you have not withheld your son, your only son, from me.*

i. *Since I first came to Pharaoh to speak in your name, he has mistreated this people.*

j. *While we were staying there for several days, a prophet named Agabus came down from Judea.*

k. *While physical training is of some value, godliness is valuable in every way.*

l. *By faith the people passed through the Red Sea as if it were dry land.*

m. *I wish I were present with you now.*

n. *Whether we are at home or away, we make it our aim to please him.*

Answers to Exercises

Chapter 1

1. Yes. The two *s* sounds are heard by English speakers as different and make a meaningful difference in pairs like *sip : ship; sow : show*.

2. *SIZE: sizes*
    LARGE: larger
    ENLARGE: enlarging
    BIG: biggest
    Even though all these words share a broad semantic domain, there are four lexemes listed under four separate lemmas. *Large* and *enlarge* share a root, but belong to different lexemes. The word *big* was not listed but *BIG* is the lemma for *biggest*.

3. *put-s, fool-ish-ness, dis-agree-ment, un-reason-able, ill-ness-es*.

4. False

5. The subject is underlined; the rest is the predicate:

    a. <u>We</u> ought to love one another.

    b. <u>I and all the people who are with me</u> will approach the city.

    c. <u>The women of the neighbourhood</u> gave him a name.

    d. Never again will there be <u>a flood</u>.

Chapter 2

1.

    a. *work; day*

    b. *she; food; kind; he*

    c. *God; people; beginning; salvation; sanctification; Spirit; faith; truth*

    d. *one; disciples; right; Jesus; place; honour*

    e. *I; you; you; me*

2.

    a. *we* (personal); *anything* (indefinite); *this* (deictic)

    b. *no-one* (negative); *who* (relative); *himself* (reflexive); *anything* (indefinite)

    c. *whom, who* (interrogative); *us* (personal)

d. *what* (interrogative); *I, I, it* (personal)

e. *this* (deictic); *it* (personal); *whoever* (indefinite); *themselves* (reflexive)

3. Direct objects are underlined; indirect objects are double underlined:

a. *The Lord will relent from his fierce anger and show <u><u>you</u></u> <u>compassion</u>.*

b. *You will not find <u>me</u>.*

c. *They heard <u>the voice</u> but saw <u>no-one</u>.*

d. *He was given <u><u>authority</u></u> over every tribe, people, language, and nation.* (The canonical sentence had *him* as indirect object, but in this indirect passive transformation *he* is the subject.) (*Tribe, people, language, nation* are complements of the preposition *over*.)

e. *His mother used to make <u><u>him</u></u> <u>a small robe</u>.*

f. *<u>The best of the flocks and cattle</u> they spared to sacrifice to the Lord.* (*Lord* is complement of the preposition *to*, though is functionally equivalent to an indirect object.)

4.

a. (*Teeth* has no verbal force, so subjective and objective genitives are out of the question.)

b. (*My* is objective)

c. *Your*

d. (*Our* is objective)

e. *Lord's*

5.

a. *which* (antecedent: *Golgotha*)

b. *whom* (antecedent: *our*, i.e. the first person plural group of writer and addressees)

c. (*Who* is interrogative.)

d. *whom* (antecedent: *Jesus, the apostle and high priest*)

e. (*That* is a conjunction.)

6.

a. (*Herself* is emphatic)

b. *yourself*

c. (*Yourself* is emphatic)

d. *themselves*

e. (*Myself* is emphatic)

Chapter 3

1.
   a. *healed; had*
   b. *prepare*
   c. *am; should go; bring*
   d. (no finite verbs)
   e. *have sinned; fall* (or: *fall short*)
   f. *thought; was; had; gave; would wait; grew* (or: *grew up*)
   g. *gather; can tell; will happen*

2.
   a. *are*
   b. *runs; continue*
   d. *sat down*
   f. *was sleeping*
   g. *are*

3.
   a. *The Spirit vindicated him.*
   b. *X opened the floodgates of the heavens.*
   c. *X will release you from service as woodcutters and water carriers.*
   d. *X is building you also, like living stones, into a spiritual house.*

4.
   a. *listening* (gerund)
   b. *wandering* (participle); *looking* (participle)
   c. *created* (participle)
   d. *hearing* (gerund)
   e. *finding* (participle)
   f. *given* (participle); *living* (participle)
   g. *walking* (gerund); *given* (participle)
   h. *coming* (gerund)

5.
   a. *will make* active indicative future perfect first singular
      want active infinitive
      to return active infinitive

b. *lift up* active imperative plural
   be lifted up passive imperative plural

c. *were washed, were sanctified, were justified* passive indicative past perfective second singular or plural

d. *had been broken off* passive indicative pluperfect perfective third plural
   were lying active indicative past imperfective third plural

e. *are* active indicative present perfective second singular or plural
   am suffering active indicative present imperfective first singular

f. *was sacrificed* passive indicative past perfective third singular
   to take away active infinitive

g. *ordered* active indicative past perfective third singular
   be given passive subjunctive present perfective third singular

Chapter 4

1.

a. *Then he gave a loaf of bread, a cake of dates and a cake of raisins to each person in the crowd of Israelites, and all the people went to their homes.*

b. *He writes the same way in all his letters, speaking in them of these matters. His letters contain some things that are hard to understand, which ignorant and unstable people distort, as they do the other Scriptures, to their own destruction.*

c. *You people of this generation, listen to what the Lord says.*

d. *Two people owed money to a certain moneylender. One owed him five hundred denarii, and the other fifty.* (*Other* is here not determining the noun *fifty*, but functioning as a noun, in fact the subject of the coordinate clause with gapped verb.)

2.

a. *great; greater; lesser*

b. *remarkable*

c. *discontented* (*All*, treated here as a determinative, would be considered an adjective in some grammars.)

d. *formless; empty*

e. *spotless, blameless and at peace with him.* (*Every*, treated here as a determinative, would be considered an adjective in some grammars.)

f. *stone*

g. *shortsighted; blind; past*

3.
   a. (*Fine* is in the predicate but modifies *child* which is also in the predicate, so is attributive.)
   b. *pleasant*
   c. (*Well* is here an adverb modifying the verb *be treated*.)
   d. *well*
   e. *beautiful*
4.
   a. *later*
   b. *directly*
   c. *faithfully*
   d. *almost*
   e. *clearly* (*Later* is elsewhere an adverb but is here an adjective modifying *times*.)
5.
   a. *rich* positive adjective, plural, used substantivally
   b. *rarely* adverb, modifying *die*
      righteous positive adjective, singular, used attributively
   c. *older; younger* comparative adjectives, singular or plural, used substantivally
   d. *only* adverb, modifying *a few*
      that deictic pronoun

Chapter 5

1.
   a. *with you*
   b. *on the face; of the earth; with seed; in it; for food*
   c. *for three days; in the desert; without finding water*
   d. *from these; over the earth; after the flood*
   e. *of you; on his shoulder; according to the number; of the tribes; of the Israelites*
   f. *among the whirling wheels; underneath the cherubim*
   g. *on the outside; to people; inside; of hypocrisy and lawlessness*

2.

a. *that (you were naked)* (subordinator) (The second *that* is a relative pronoun.)

b. *whether* (subordinator)

c. *and* (coordinator); *or* (coordinator); *but* (coordinator) (*If* would be treated by some grammars as a subordinating conjunction. *How* is sometimes a subordinator, but is here an interrogative adverb.)

d. *Yet* (coordinator); *and* (coordinator);

e. *that (I did not run)* (subordinator); *nor* (coordinator); (*So that* in some grammars would be treated as a subordinating conjunction).

Chapter 6

1.

a. *X found someone who was worthy to open the scroll and to look into it.*

b. *My time has now come.*

c. *I was a burden to someone* (or *X*).

d. *There is a sword or spear here at your disposal.*

e. *This means x.*

f. *X knows such things as these.*

g. *You have laid him at x place.*

h. *You stand here for x reason.*

2.

a. Closed; expects answer *No.*

b. Closed; expects answer *Yes.*

c. Open.

d. Closed; expects answer *No.*

e. Open.

f. Closed; neutral (as far as we can tell).

g. Closed; expects answer *No.*

h. Closed; speaker believes answer should be *Yes.*

Chapter 7

1.

a. *to show them a sign from heaven* infinitive-clause, content (directive)

b. *by finishing the work* gerund-clause, adverbial (manner)

c. *your coming; your going* gerund-clauses, content

d. *those living in the valleys* participial clause, relative

e. *Having been warned in a dream* participial clause, adverbial (temporal)
   not to go back to Herod infinitive-clause, content (directive)

2.

a. *that you have done this with a clear conscience* content

b. *what makes him so strong* content (open question)
   how we can subdue him content (open question)

c. *so that no one ... would kill him* adverbial (purpose)
   who came upon him relative

d. *so that the land was filled with them* adverbial (result)

e. *that he is very cunning* content

f. *how I will find out* content (open question)
   if you are honest men adverbial (condition)

g. *were I to count them* adverbial (condition)

h. *that you fear God* content
   since you have not withheld your son, your only son
   from me adverbial (reason)

i. *since I first came to Pharaoh* adverbial (temporal)

j. *while we were staying there for several days* adverbial (temporal)

k. *while physical training is of some value* adverbial (concession)

l. *as if it were dry land* adverbial (comparison)

m. *I were present with you now* content

n. *Whether we are at home or away* adverbial (condition)

Index

past-participle form 48
past time 55
perfective 65
perfect tense 56
periphrastic 44
person 32
personal pronoun 31
phoneme 8
phonology 8
phrase 19
pluperfect 56
positive 77
possessive case 28
postpositive 79
predicate 16
predicative adjective 80
predicative complement 42
predicative genitive 29
predicative nominative 27
predicator 16, 39
prefix 13
preposition 89
prepositional complement 30, 90
prepositional verb 44
present perfect 56
present time 55
preterite 48
pronoun 22
proper adjective 73
proper noun 22
protasis 115
proximal 33
purpose clause 114

Q

question 97

R

reason clause 113
reciprocal pronoun 36
referent 9
reflexive pronoun 34
register 12
relative clause 109

relative pronoun 35
result clause 114
root 10
rule (grammatical) 12

S

semantic domain 9
semantics 9
sentence 19
simple form 47
subject 16
subjective genitive 28
subjunctive 53, 108
subordinate clause 104
subordinator 93
substantival adjective 81
substantival participle 63
suffix 13
superlative 78
supplementation 104
syntax 15

T

temporal clause 112
tense 55
to-infinitive 57
transformation 19
transitive 46

V

verb 39
verbal adjective 74
verbal aspect 64
verbal noun 57
vocative case 30
voice 49
vowel 8